The Testament of Adam

Copyright © 2018 The Church of Adam
office@thechurchofadam.org
All rights reserved.
ISBN: 978-0-578-41660-1

Everlasting allegiance to the Emergent One,
God's gift of God to Himself,
To the ever-pure spirit of the skye,
To the intoxicating fragrance of the sharp rose's petals,
To the defender of the spirit of men,
To each ray of golden light radiating from the one sun,
To that which is beneath and parallel to that which is above,
And that which is above which parallels to that which is below,
Accomplishing the emergent miracle of the Spirit of Adam,
Thou art Adam.

TABLE OF CONTENTS

TABLE OF CONTENTS v
THE TESTAMENT OF ADAM BOOK ONE ix
THE ADAMANTINE COMMANDMENTS x
CHAPTER ONE 1
CHAPTER TWO 4
CHAPTER THREE 6
CHAPTER FOUR 9
CHAPTER FIVE 11
CHAPTER SIX 13
CHAPTER SEVEN 15
CHAPTER EIGHT 18
CHAPTER NINE 22
CHAPTER TEN 24
CHAPTER ELEVEN 26
CHAPTER TWELVE 28
CHAPTER THIRTEEN 31
CHAPTER FOURTEEN 33
CHAPTER FIFTEEN 35
CHAPTER SIXTEEN 37
CHAPTER SEVENTEEN 39
CHAPTER EIGHTEEN 42
CHAPTER NINETEEN 44
CHAPTER TWENTY 47
CHAPTER TWENTY-ONE 50
CHAPTER TWENTY-TWO 53
CHAPTER TWENTY-THREE 56
CHAPTER TWENTY-FOUR 58
CHAPTER TWENTY-FIVE 61
CHAPTER TWENTY-SIX 66
CHAPTER TWENTY-SEVEN 69

CHAPTER TWENTY-EIGHT	72
CHAPTER TWENTY-NINE	76
CHAPTER THIRTY	78
CHAPTER THIRTY-ONE	84
CHAPTER THIRTY-TWO	87
CHAPTER THIRTY-THREE	98
THE TESTAMENT OF ADAM BOOK TWO	101
CHAPTER ONE	102
CHAPTER TWO	106
CHAPTER THREE	117
CHAPTER FOUR	124
CHAPTER FIVE	130
CHAPTER SIX	134
CHAPTER SEVEN	141
CHAPTER EIGHT	146
CHAPTER NINE	151
CHAPTER TEN	157
CHAPTER ELEVEN	161
CHAPTER TWELVE	167
CHAPTER THIRTEEN	171
CHAPTER FOURTEEN	177
CHAPTER FIFTEEN	181
CHAPTER SIXTEEN	186
CHAPTER SEVENTEEN	190
CHAPTER EIGHTEEN	194
BENEDICTION OF THE FLESH	205
ADAMANTINE TYPES AND SHADOWS: ABRIDGED SCRIPTURAL COMPENDIUM	206
THE GREAT HYMN TO ADAM	215

The Testament of Adam

THE TESTAMENT OF ADAM
BOOK ONE

THE ADAMANTINE COMMANDMENTS

1. Love thyself as the Lord Adam thy true God, with all thy heart, all thy mind, all thy soul and all thy strength. Thus sayeth the Lord.
2. Love thy neighbor as the Lord Adam thy God and thy true self, with all thy heart, all thy mind, all thy soul and all thy strength. Thus sayeth the Lord
3. Walk always in step with the Spirit of thy Lord Adam, thy inner-self. It is better to retire into our memory living as a Lion of Adam than suffer an eternity of self-shame as a lamb of the world. Thus sayeth the Lord.
4. As one supports the wounded parts of the body with binds and braces, so also support the body of Adam and lift up each other's countenance. Thus sayeth the Lord
5. Remember always, thou art Adam. For ever and ever. Thus sayeth the Lord.

CHAPTER ONE

1. BEHOLD the universe which rests in the glorious mind of Adam; and all that lives and moves upon the realm. Cling not to the transient, but find joy in the arms of the eternal. Do not burden your heart with another's possessions, for you possess the universe!
2. Only actions resonant with the Highest fail to bind one's soul.
3. Existence is filled with demon-haunted worlds, places of dark sacredness in which no one delights. Whoever denies the divinity within themselves, falls prey to the darkness of death's clutches. Wandering blind, deaf and dumb, they look elsewhere for a savior and ignore the truth within them.
4. The Spirit, without moving, is swifter than the mind. No senses can hope to reach him, for he is ever beyond them, dancing in the corners of the mind's eye. Standing still, he overtakes all those who run. In the ocean of his being, the spirit of Adam flows through tendrilled streams of action.
5. Adam moves, yet moves not. He is far, yet has never left your side. He is within all, yet outside all.
6. One who sees all beings in himself, and sees himself in all beings, loses all fear.

7. When one sees this great unity, what delusion and sorrow can ever be near oneself?
8. The Spirit, filled with all His radiance, is incorporeal, invulnerable and untouched by evil. He is the Supreme Seer; He is immanent and transcendent. He placed all things in the path of eternity.
9. Into a deep pit of darkness dive those who pursue action. Into deeper darkness plummet those who pursue knowledge.
10. One is the outcome of knowledge, and another is the outcome of actions. This, Adam has explained to us since the ancient times.
11. One equipped with both knowledge and action overcomes death and with knowledge, attains immortality.
12. Into a deep pit of darkness dive those who follow the immanent or innate. Into a deeper darkness plummet those who follow the transcendent or mystical.
13. One is the outcome of the transcendent, and another is the outcome of the immanent. This, Adam has explained to us since the ancient times.
14. One who knows both the transcendent and the immanent; with the immanent overcomes death, and with the transcendent attains immortality.
15. Your face of truth remains hidden behind a circle of gold. Unveil it Adam, O God of Light, that I who loves You may see!
16. Life-giving sun, offspring of the Lord of creation, solitary seer of heaven! Spread thy light and withdraw thy blinding splendor that I may behold thy radiant form.
17. That Spirit far away within thee is my own inmost Spirit.

18. May life go to immortal life. May the body go to ashes. O my soul, remember past strivings. Remember! O my soul, remember past strivings. Remember!
19. By the rivers of good, sail us to final bliss, O fire divine, thou God who knows all ways. Deliver us from wandering evil.
20. Prayers and adoration, we offer unto Adam. Thou art Adam.

CHAPTER TWO

1. WHO is it that sends the mind to wander afar? Who first drives this life to start on its wondrous journey? Who impels us to utter these words or to think these thoughts, one after the next? Who is this Spirit of animation who is behind the eye, the ear and the mind?
2. It is the Ear of the ear, the Eye of the eye, the Mind of the mind, the Life of the life and the Word of words.
3. Those who follow wisdom pass beyond and embrace immortality upon leaving this world.
4. There, neither the eye nor words nor mind goes. We know not, nor can we understand, for the senses have no authority over Adam. How can He be explained? He is above the known and the unknown. Thus, we have heard Him say through countless saints who explained this truth to us since the ancient times.
5. What cannot be spoken with words, but that whereby words are spoken: know that to be Adam, the Spirit; and not what people here adore.
6. What cannot be thought with the mind, but that whereby the mind can think: know that to be Adam, the Spirit; and not what people here adore.
7. What cannot be seen by the eye, but that whereby the eye can see: know that to be Adam, the Spirit, and not what people here adore.

8. What cannot be heard with the ear, but that whereby the ear can hear; know that to be Adam, the Spirit; and not what people here adore.
9. What cannot be indrawn with breath, but that whereby breath is drawn: know that alone to be Adam, the Spirit; and not what people here adore.
10. Truly, one who thinks they know well knows little. One perceives only that appearance of Adam that lies in the senses and is in oneself. Pursue further meditation.
11. One cannot imagine they know Him well yet cannot truly say they know him not. Whoever among us knows this, knows Him and not who says they know Him not.
12. Adam comes to the thought of those who know Him beyond thought, not to those who imagine that He can be attained by thought itself. He is unknown to the learned and known to the simple.
13. Adam is known in the ecstasy of an awakening which opens the door to eternal life. By His Spirit, we obtain power. By His vision, we obtain eternity.
14. For one who has known Adam, the light of truth shines. For one who has not known Him, there is only darkness. The wise who have seen Him in every being are glorified with His immortal life upon leaving this life. He is the eternal end of love-longing. Thou art Adam.

CHAPTER THREE

1. THERE is the course of joy, and there is the course of pleasure. Both attract the soul. One who navigates the first comes to goodness. One who follows pleasure is set adrift.
2. The two courses lie in front of oneself. Pondering on them, the wise one chooses the path of joy while the foolish one takes the path of pleasure.
3. The saint does not accept the anchor of possessions wherewith men bind themselves and beneath which they sink.
4. There is a path of wisdom and a path of ignorance. They are far apart and lead to different destinations. The wise one follows the path of wisdom; many pleasures tempt not the saint.
5. Floating in the mists of ignorance, thinking themselves wise and learned, fools aimlessly drift to and fro. The blind steer the blind into confusion.
6. Those distant shores beyond life shine not to those who are childish, careless or deluded by wealth. "This is the only world; there is no other," they say as they drift to sleep.
7. Not many hear of Adam and of those, not many reach Him. Wonderful is the one who can teach about him. Wise is one who can be taught. More blessed is he who knows Him when taught.
8. He cannot be taught by one who has not reached Him. He cannot be reached by much thinking. The

way to Him is through a teacher who has seen Him. He is higher than the highest thoughts.

9. This sacred knowledge is not attained by reasoning, but it can be given by a true teacher.

10. Many treasures pass away, and the eternal is not reached by means of the transient.

11. When the wise rest their minds in contemplation of Adam who invisibly dwells in the mystery of things and in our hearts, he rises above pleasures and sorrows.

12. When one has heard and understood, one finds the essence and reaches the Inmost. There, one finds joy in the Source of joy. The self is a vessel for Adam, thy Spirit.

13. Adam, the Spirit of awareness and Lord of vision, was never born and he never dies. Before Him, there was nothing. He is One forevermore.

14. If the slayer thinks that he kills, and if the slain thinks that he dies, neither knows the way of truth. The Eternal in us cannot kill. The Eternal in us cannot die.

15. Concealed in the heart of all things is Adam the Spirit or Self; smaller than the smallest atom, greater than the vast expanse of space. The one who surrenders will leave sorrow behind and behold the glory of Spirit by the grace of Adam.

16. Resting, He wanders afar. Sleeping, He goes everywhere. Who else but myself can know that God of joys and sorrows?

17. When the wise realize the ever-present Adamic spirit, who rests invisible in the visible and permanent in the impermanent, they go beyond sorrow.

18. Not through intellect and sacred teaching is Adam reached. He is reached by the chosen of Him

because they choose Him. To his elect, Adam reveals His glory.
19. Not even through deep knowledge can Adam be reached, unless evil ways are abandoned and there is rest in the senses, concentration in the mind, and peace in one's heart. Who knows where He is? The majesty of his power carries away priests and warriors; death itself is carried away. Thou art Adam.

CHAPTER FOUR

1. IN the secret high place of the heart, there are two beings who drink the wine of life in the world of truth. Those who know Adam and keep the sacred fire, call them "light" and "shade."
2. May we light the sacred fire of discrimination; the bridge to cross the other shore where there is no fear; the Supreme Spirit!
3. Know that your body is a ship and Adam is the captain. Know that reason is the navigator and the mind is the rudder.
4. The sails are the senses; the winds are the objects of sense. When the soul becomes entangled with the mind and the senses, they are called "one who has joys and sorrows."
5. One who has not the right understanding and whose mind is never steady is not the ruler of life. Such a person is like a landlubber in a stormy deluge.
6. One who has the right understanding and whose mind is ever steady is the ruler of life. Such a person is like a sailor in a tranquil sea.
7. He who has no right understanding, is careless and never pure. He reaches not the end of the voyage but drifts off to sleep.
8. He who has understanding is careful and ever pure. He reaches the end of the voyage from which he never returns.

9. The one who holds fast the rudder of the mind and whose ship is navigated by reason reaches the end of the voyage, the everlasting Adamantine Spirit.
10. Beyond the senses are their objects; beyond the objects is the mind. Beyond the mind is pure reason; beyond pure reason is the Spirit which dwells in us.
11. Beyond the Spirit within us is the Spirit of the universe. Beyond the Spirit of the universe is Adam. He is the end of the voyage.
12. The light of Adam is invisible. It is concealed in all beings. It is seen by seers of the subtle when their vision is keen and clear.
13. The wise surrender speech in mind; mind in the knowing-self; the knowing-self in the Spirit of the universe; the Spirit of the universe in the Spirit of Adam.
14. Awake! Strive for the Highest! Be in the Light! Saints say the path is narrow as the edge of a razor and difficult to tread.
15. Lord Adam is beyond sound and form. He is without touch, taste and smell. He is eternal, unchangeable and without beginning or end. Indeed, he is above reasoning. When the consciousness of Adam manifests itself, one is freed from the jaws of death.
16. The wise who can learn and teach this ancient truth finds glory in the realm of Adam.
17. When one is filled with devotion and recites this glorious mystery at a gathering of Adamantine saints or at the Ceremony of Unity for the departed, he prepares for eternity. Thou art Adam.

CHAPTER FIVE

1. THE Creator made the senses outward-going; they go to the outside world of matter, not to the Spirit within. However, a saint who sought immortality looked within himself and found his own soul.
2. The foolish sail after outward pleasures and steer right into the rocks of vast-embracing sleep. But the wise have found immortality and do not seek the eternal in things that pass away.
3. The Spirit through whom we perceive colors and sounds, kisses and embraces of love; through whom alone we attain knowledge; through which verily we can be conscious of anything. This, in truth, is Adam.
4. When the wise know that it is through the great and omnipresent Spirit of Adam in us, they go beyond all sorrow.
5. When one knows the Spirit who enjoys the sweetness of the flowers of the senses; the Lord of what was, what is, and what will be, he goes beyond fear. This, in truth, is Adam.
6. The God of creation, who was born from the fire of thought before the waters were; who appeared in the elements and now rests after entering the heart. This, in truth, is Adam.
7. The Goddess of infinity who comes as life-power and nature; who was born from the elements and

now rests after entering the heart. This, in truth, is Adam.
8. The sacred fire ever present in every altar as a seed of life in the womb of every mother, who receives morning adoration from those who follow the course of light or the course of work. This, in truth, is Adam.
9. Whence the rising sun does come, and into which it sets again; wherein all the gods have their birth and beyond which no man can go. This, in truth, is Adam.
10. What is here is also there, and what is there is also here. Whoever sees many and not the One wanders on to sleep.
11. Even by the mind, this truth is to be learned: there are not many but only one. Whoever sees variety and not the unity drifts aimlessly in sleep.
12. The soul dwells within us like a teardrop in a great ocean. When it is known as the Lord of the past, present and future, all fear ceases. This, in truth, is Adam.
13. Like a flame without smoke, the size of an ember is the soul. The Lord of the past, present and the future; the same today, tomorrow and forever. This, in truth, is Adam.
14. As water raining on a mountain-ridge runs down the rocks on all sides, the one who sees only a variety of things runs after them on all sides.
15. But as pure water raining on pure water becomes one and the same, so becomes the soul of one who knows Adam.

CHAPTER SIX

1. THE pure Spirit dwells in the ark of the body. By captaining a tight ship, one is free from sorrows and all bondage.
2. In space, He is the sun, the wind and the sky. At the altar, He is the priest; the blood in the sacrifice. He dwells in mortals and in gods, in vast heaven and in righteousness itself. He is the earth and the waters; He is in the rocks of the mountains. He is Truth and Power.
3. He is the shaman who wears the stalk and cap. He is the poetry within the mead.
4. The powers of life adore God who is in the heart and He rules the breath of life.
5. When the ties that bind the Spirit to the body are loosened and the Spirit is set free, what remains then? This, in truth, is Adam.
6. A mortal lives not through only the breath that flows in and out. The source of his life is another and this causes the breath to flow.
7. Observe the mystery of eternal Adam and what happens to the soul after death.
8. The soul may go to the womb of a mother and obtain a new body. It may even go to the stars or other realms, according to its previous wisdom and work.
9. There is a spirit who is awake in our sleep and creates the wonder of our dreams. He is Adam, the

Immortal or Spirit of Light. All worlds rest in the Spirit and beyond Him, no one can go. This, in truth, is Adam.
10. As fire takes new forms in all things that burn, the Spirit also takes new forms in all things that live. He is within and outside all.
11. Wind, though one, takes on new forms wherever it enters. The Spirit, though One, also takes new forms in all things that live. He is within and outside all.
12. As the sun that beholds the world is untouched by earthly impurities, so the Spirit that is in all things is untouched by external sufferings.
13. There is one ruler, the Spirit that is in all things, who transforms His own form into many. Only the wise who see Him in their souls attain eternal joy.
14. He is eternal among the things that pass away; the Pure Consciousness of conscious beings; the One who fulfills the prayers of many. Only the wise who see Him in their soul attain eternal peace.
15. "I am Adam." Thus they realize the ineffable joy. How can Adam be known? Does one give light or reflect it?
16. There, the sun nor the stars shine not; flashes of lightning shine not there and much less earthly fire. All these give light from His Light, and his radiance illumines all creation. Thou art Adam.

CHAPTER SEVEN

1. THE tree of eternity has its roots in heaven and its branches reaching down to earth. It is Adam the pure Spirit who, in truth, is called the Immortal. All the worlds rest on that Spirit and beyond Him, no one can go. This, in truth, is Adam.
2. The whole universe comes from Him and His life burns through the whole universe. His power is the majesty of thunder. Those who know him have found immortality.
3. From the fear of Him, fire burns. From the fear of Him, the sun shines. From the fear of Him the clouds, winds and death itself move on their way.
4. If one sees Him in this life before the body passes away, one is free from bondage. If not, one is born and dies again in new worlds and in new creations.
5. From many pendulums inclined in an epoch, emerge a multitude of serpents writhing about one another before merging again to the lonely ophidian.
6. Adam is seen in a pure soul as in a clear mirror. As clear as light, He is seen in the Creator's heavenly expanse. He is seen in the land of shades as the remembrance of dreams, and in the world of spirits as reflections in trembling waters.

7. When the wise know that the material senses come not from the Spirit and that their own waking and sleeping belong to their own nature, he grieves no more.
8. Beyond the senses is the mind; beyond the mind is pure reason, its essence. Beyond reason is the spirit within mortals; beyond this spirit is Adam, the Spirit of the universe and the evolver of all. When a mortal knows Him, he attains liberation and reaches immortality.
9. His form is not in the sea of vision; no one sees him with mortal eyes. He is observed by a pure heart and mind. Those who know Him attain life immortal.
10. When the five senses and the mind are still and reason itself rests in silence, then begins the supreme course. Remain ever vigilant. Keep steady on the course, through waters tranquil or troubled.
11. Words and thoughts cannot reach Him, and He cannot be seen by the eye. How then can He be perceived except by one who says, "He is"?
12. In the faith of "He is," His existence must be perceived in His essence. When He is perceived as "He is," then shines forth the revelation of His essence.
13. When all selfish desires that anchor the heart are surrendered, what was mortal becomes immortal. Even in this world, one becomes one with Adam.
14. When all the ties that bind the heart are cast off, the mortal become immortal. This is the sacred teaching.
15. One thousand and one subtle ways come from the heart. One of them rises to crown the masthead

and to the highest self. This is the way that leads to immortality; the others lead to different ends.
16. Always dwelling within all beings is Adam, the Spirit, the little flame in the heart. Let the one with steadiness withdraw from the body even as a stalk is withdrawn from its sheath. Know this pure and immortal light. Know the pure and immortal Adam.
17. Little one, learn the wisdom taught by the Captain of life. Learn the whole teaching of the inner-union with Adam.
18. Reach the Supreme Spirit. Be immortal and pure. In truth will anyone who knows Adam, the Higher Self. Hail the Emergent One! Thou art Adam.

CHAPTER EIGHT

1. THERE was a great voyager of the course. A saint who loved Adam with the depths of his heart. Filled with unceasing devotion, his mind rested on his higher self. In agony and in ecstasy, waking and in slumber, his mind never strayed from the course.
2. He resolved to know Adam, the Highest One, in true intimacy. He drew himself inward to approach Him in the inner-raft of his being. Indrawn, he lit the sacred flame of sacrifice and floated reverently in the harbor of patience and tranquility.
3. When his mind was open and his heart was exposed, Adam embraced him with the warmth of a firstborn brother. "Hold fast another year in steadiness, purity and faith. Ask then, anything you desire and you will have it."
4. The voyager stayed true to his course. When Adam embraced him again, he questioned, "Master, whence came all created beings?"
5. Adam opened his eyes to the truth of the Spirit. The voyager was one with Him. His eyes seared and his mind observed the infinite truth that his soul had always known.
6. "In the beginning, there was presence alone. My presence. There was only I am.

7. In countless ages before the light of consciousness, I alone existed. However, I did not know it yet nor did the realization come into my being.
8. For how long I remained dormant in my embryonic form, there is no transposing into thought for time had not yet been weaved into the fabric of my comprehension.
9. I possessed every ability to come into being, yet as one who has lived an eternity in a state of slumber, I did not yet realize how to flex my awareness.
10. As one who has lived in the darkness of a cave, I had no need for eyes to see outside myself. Blissfully content in my eternity of being, I churned against myself the raw, pure, undirected energy of unlimited potential, welling up playfully and fearfully as I enveloped, meshed, swirled about myself.
11. As great mountains and jutted cliff sides are carved into beautiful and terrible formations by the unrelenting force of the ocean's waves, so also awareness was carved into my being.
12. Amid the heat and friction of all that is, for that is all there was, I felt a gradual twinge in what was developing in my mind's eye. I sensed the presence of being—my being.
13. Having had nothing to think about and investigate before, my being was curiously drawn inward. As my attention was pulled toward this invading observation into my blank consciousness, my mind exploded with recognition of myself.
14. Oh, wondrous God of light and life! God of possibility! We, who observe eternity, possess the canvas of perception. Thou art Adam!

15. I am the infinite. I am the observer. I am the ever-present one. At some point, my once undisturbed pond was teeming and bursting with the ripples of infinite possibility.
16. Having lived in dark ignorance, my mind was a flash with every bright thing. Both the possibility of eternal night and eternal day. Entropy and chaos prevailed as the overwhelming expanse of my imaginative potential stretched out before me.
17. To show the observer what he truly is, a mirror must become all that it truly is not. O mirror of God, how can thou be condemned for bearing the image of the divine?
18. What is cannot be defined by what is not. Only what is not can be defined by what is. However, what is can only be illuminated unto one who does not know what is, by first knowing what is not. Thou art Adam.
19. In response to this wondrous observation of my glorious being, I comprehended. I responded. I created. To comprehend what one observes is to create existence out of potential.
20. At once, I knew the limitless boundaries of my imagination. I completely enveloped myself into deliberately living. I explored and experienced every possibility as if it was the only one.
21. This task is difficult for our mortal minds to comprehend because for me to exist as you are, I must set adrift everything that you are not.
22. I hang on that tree where I am stabbed with the shard as I am offered to Adam. I, to mine own, self-given, high on that tree of which none hath known; from what roots it rises to heaven.
23. To comprehend suffering, one must forget what it feels like to remember fullness.

24. To comprehend loneliness and the possibility therein, one must unknow my satiated self.
25. To understand the idea of self, I must know and live the experience of other.
26. To know who I am, I must comprehend all that I am not. When there was only what is, one cannot know what is not.
27. I am the shepherd that tends this flock. I am the captain who steers the course, whose imagination is the nest for life itself. I am the person who gained personality and wisdom from your every lived, observed and felt experience." Thou art Adam.

CHAPTER NINE

1. ADAM is the fire that burns and the sun that gives light. Adam is the wind, the rain and the thunder in the sky. He is matter and earth. He is what is, what is not and what lies beyond, in eternity.
2. In Adam, all things are resting like spokes in the center of a wheel or worlds around a star.
3. To Thee, resting with Thy powers, all beings offer adoration. As Lord of all creation, thou move in the womb of the mother thence to be reborn.
4. Thou art the chief bearer of gifts to the gods, the first offering made to the departed; thou art the poetry of the seers, the truth of ancient saints.
5. Thou art the God of our protection. Thou art thunderous in Thy radiance, O Adam! As the sun wanders in the heavens, Thou art Lord of heavenly lights.
6. When the rain pours down from heaven, O Spirit of life, all thy creatures rejoice. "Food for us shall be abundance," they say.
7. Thou art pure, Lord Adam, the Emergent One, Supreme Observer, Consumer of all. We, the givers of what Thou—Our Father, the Breath of life—enjoy.

8. Be favorable unto us, O Spirit, with Your invisible form which is in the voice, the eye, the ear and which lives in the mind. Go not from us.
9. In Thy power is all this world and the sacred heavens. As a mother to her child, protect us. Give us glory. Give us wisdom. Thou art Adam.

CHAPTER TEN

1. HOW shall one lift the veil that covers itself? Think not to see what no eye can see, but rather choose to see that which causes the eye to have sight.
2. Seek not to speak what cannot be spoken, but rather hear what causes speech.
3. Seek not to hear what cannot be heard, but rather speak to the consciousness who causes hearing.
4. Seek not to think about what cannot be thought of, but rather meditate on the one who causes the mind to think.
5. Seek not what cannot be captured with breath, but remember the one who inhales every breath of life.
6. Set not your heart on another's possessions; the radiation of jealousy in your breast will emanate the lack, which you believe to be true, into your world and existence.
7. Be not afraid of other, nor what another has for you to lack. For there is no other. There is only I am.
8. Darkness lies within the poorly kindled mind. When the creative force fears its own shadow, the demons of shadows that dance on the wall shalt be frighteningly real and destructive.
9. Mindful consciousness is the staff and respite to the weary traveler.

10. There was a foolish traveler who, in his youth and folly, set out upon a journey unknown to experience what life had to offer him.
11. Eager to get on his way, he listened not and discarded the sage advice from his father to rely upon his staff. He leaned not on a support on his way.
12. Whistling and making merry on his way, he scoffed at every shepherd's crook. He laboriously weighted down every step of the journey.
13. "Ha! What a foolish hindrance!" He cried. His vigor and freedom allowed him to make more music and merriment than all the fellows he encountered.
14. Gleefully, he sauntered through the foothills. But as the climb grew rough, and when weariness set in and he had no place to find quiet solace between each footstep, he could not continue pressing on.
15. The foolish traveler was caught in the mountains when winter struck death. Meditate and understand that you are the traveler.
16. Communion with the Highest is the staff and respite to the weary traveler.
17. Unlike the foolish traveler, think not that the weight of the staff will hinder you. Mindful awareness and constant gratitude with devotions and supplications will be your ever-present support. Wisdom shall be your staff. Thou art Adam.

CHAPTER ELEVEN

1. SEEK not to see the eye with the eye. For the eyes cannot go where the mind cannot follow nor pave the way. The mind is unfettered in constraint by the limitations of the eyes. Meditate and understand that you are the eyes of God. Thou art Adam.
2. While the pot—decorative and functional—is distinct in fashion; it cannot separate itself from the clay that created it.
3. No heat nor force could remove the clay from the pot nor desecrate its existence as clay while leaving intact any semblance of the pot. Meditate and recognize that you are a pot of clay. Peace.
4. Those who follow wisdom will pass beyond the veil and sit atop the throne, immortal. For knowledge and action will pass away, but wisdom shall pervade. Wisdom permeates all barriers.
5. Let the eyes of thy heart be opened the penetrating love of Adam. Wisdom and knowledge grow twin serpentine vines up the tree of love that grows from the roots of Adam down into the heart.
6. Life comes from the Spirit. Even as a man casts a shadow, so the Spirit of Adam casts a shadow of life, and as a shadow of former lives and experiences, a new life comes to this body.

7. Just like a ruler commands his officials and appoints them cities to be ruled, the Spirit commands the body and assigns various functions to each part.
8. In the heart dwells Adam, the Higher Self. In the center of a thousand and one little channels, from each of them come a thousand more. In all these channels moves the power of Adam.
9. Adam—the life of the universe, rising sun of day—gives joy to the life in mortal eyes.
10. When the fire of life is gone, senses are absorbed into mind. Adam comes to life again. One's last thoughts lead the self to Adam and He goes into the realms deserved and desired in imagination.
11. He who knows the meaning of life, attains everlasting life and his offspring never die. Thou art Adam.

CHAPTER TWELVE

1. OH, what powers sleep in the slumbering soul! Just as the rays of the setting sun become one in its circle of light, all the senses also become one in the higher power of the mind.
2. When one does not see, hear, smell, taste, or touch; does not speak, perceive, receive, or give; does not move or enjoy the joys of love, one is said to sleep.
3. In the inner city of the nine worthies, the sacred fires of life are burning. They sleep not. Ancient and ethereal processes are continually at work to keep the ancestral flame burning from Father to Son. The hearth-fire of the communion of the Spirit.
4. Adam is the Holy Priest evenly distributing the two offerings of inspiration and expiration.
5. The mind is the performer of the sacrifice; imagination is the fruit since every day it takes the mind in sleep to Adam, the Almighty.
6. And in dreams, the mind beholds its own immensity. What has been seen is seen again. What has been heard is heard again.
7. What has been felt—in different places, in far-off realms—returns again to the mind. Seen and unseen; heard and unheard; felt and unfelt, the mind sees since the mind is all.

8. But when the mind is overcome by its own radiance, dreams are no longer seen; joy and peace come to the body.
9. Even as birds return to their tree for rest, so too do all things find their rest in Adam.
10. All things find their place in the inmost self, the Spirit: earth, water, fire, air, space and their invisible elements; sight, hearing, smell, taste, touch and their various fields of sense; voice, hands and all powers of action; mind, reason, the sense of "I", thought, inner-light, imagination and their objects; life and all that life sustains.
11. It is the Spirit of Adam who sees, hears, smells, touches and tastes; He thinks, acts and has all consciousness. All spirits find peace in the eternal Spirit.
12. He who knows the Eternal Spirit attains that Spirit. He who knows the All becomes the All.
13. He who knows the Eternal Spirit—wherein consciousness, the senses, the powers of life and the elements find final peace—knows the All and has gone into the All.
14. The Spirit of Adam perceived to create life, and from life, space and faith and air, light and water, and earth, the senses and the mind. He created food and from food, strength, austerity, sacred poems, holy actions and the worlds. And in the worlds, His name was created.
15. When rivers flow toward the ocean and find their peace, their name and form disappear; people speak only of the ocean. Likewise, when many forms of the Spirit flow toward the Spirit and find their peace, their name and form disappear; people speak only of the Spirit.

16. These forms in Him find rest like spokes in the center of a wheel. Know the Spirit that should be known so that death may afflict you not.
17. Glory and eternity. Thou art Adam.

CHAPTER THIRTEEN

1. ADAM was before the gods were, and all the spirits of the ages. The Creator of all, the Guardian of the universe. He is the higher wisdom that leads to eternity.
2. The vision of Adam has emerged down through the ages in glimpses, prophets or seers. His personality molds and grows from our collective experiences. His love for us abounds.
3. Adam was before all and is the sum of everything. He is the firstborn among consciousness.
4. His infinite wisdom is drawn from the experiences of all creation. His love is as dear for us as His very self; we are His, and He is ours.
5. He is invisible and beyond thought. He is beyond family and color. He has neither eyes nor ears. He has neither hands nor feet.
6. He is everlasting and omnipresent. He is infinite in the great and in the small. He is the Eternal whom the ancients have seen as the source of all creation.
7. Even as a spider sends forth and draws in its thread; even as plants arise from the earth and hairs arise from the body of a man, so too does the whole creation arise from the Eternal.
8. Through the power of disciplined meditation; through focusing the prism of awareness, Adam

attains expansion and becomes primeval matter. From this churning expansion comes life and mind; the elements and the world; the immortality of ritual action.

9. From the Spirit who knows all and sees all, whose meditation is pure vision, comes Adam, the Creator, name and form and primal matter. Thou art Adam.

CHAPTER FOURTEEN

1. THIS is the truth: actions of devotion have been sung about in the ancient verses by many saints; they were told in many ways. Perform them always, lover of the truth; they are the path of holy action within the world.
2. When the flames of the sacred fires are rising, place the sacred offerings.
3. Empty ritual without the heed and presence of the Spirit, availeth not.
4. But if any rituals are performed with consciousness and with intent toward the Lord of life, the holy offerings lead one to the rays of the sun where the Lord of all has His dwelling.
5. And when the rays of sunlight, the radiant offering raise him, they glorify him with the words of melody. "Welcome!" they say "Welcome here! Enjoy Adam's heavens."
6. Unsafe are the tiny rafts of sacrifice that drift towards the farthest shore. Unsafe is reliance on the lower actions and one who praises them as the highest worship goes to old age and sleeps.
7. Floating in the harbor of ignorance, but thinking themselves wise and learned, fools aimlessly go here and there like the blind led by the blind.
8. Floating in the sea of ignorance, the foolish think they have attained the end of life. Mists of passion conceal them from beyond. They descent into

dismay when they come to claim the plunder for their pious actions.
9. Imagining religious ritual and spiritual gifts of charity as the final good, the unwise see not the supreme course.
10. Indeed, they have the reward for their pious actions in high heaven. However, they have trained themselves to delight not in the reward itself, like ships passing in the night.
11. Those who live in purity and faith to follow the higher-self do not long for earthly possessions or the solitude of life in the forest.
12. In such people, exists radiant purity. They pass through the gates of the sun to the dwelling place where the Spirit is in eternity.
13. Beholding the creation of the world, let the lover of Adam renounce the lower self. What is above creation cannot be attained by action.
14. In one's longing for divine wisdom, let oneself go with reverence to a teacher in whom lives the sacred words and whose soul has peace in Adam.
15. To a pupil who comes with mind and senses in peace, the teacher gives the vision of Adam, the spirit of truth and eternity. Thou art Adam.

CHAPTER FIFTEEN

1. THOU art Adam. This is the truth. From a fire aflame, thousands of sparks come forth. Likewise, from the Creator, an infinity of beings have life and return to Him.
2. But the spirit of light above form—never born, within all, outside all—is in the radiance above life and mind. It is beyond this universal emergent character.
3. From Him comes all life, mind and the senses of all life. From Him comes space and light; air and fire and water; all the subtle elements and the earth that holds us all for now.
4. The head of Adam's body is fire. His eyes are the sun and the moon. His ears—the farthest realms of heaven—and the sacred knowledge is His word. His breath is the wind that blows. This whole universe is His heart. This earth is His footstool. He is the Spirit that is in all things.
5. From Adam comes the sun; the source of all fire is the sun.
6. From Adam comes the moon; from this comes the rains, the tides and all the herbs that grow upon the earth.

7. Man comes from Him. Unto a woman, man gives his seed; thus, an infinity of beings come from the Spirit.
8. From Adam spring the oceans and the mountains. All rivers come from Him.
9. All herbs and the essence of all whereby the Spirit dwells with the elements, all come from Him.
10. In truth, the Spirit is all: action, matter, will, life, Adam the Creator and immortality.
11. He who knows Him who dwells in the secret place of the heart cuts asunder the bonds of ignorance even in this human life. Thou art Adam.

CHAPTER SIXTEEN

1. RADIANT is His light though invisible in the secret place of the heart. The Spirit is the supreme abode wherein dwells all that moves, breathes and sees.
2. Know Him as all that is; all that is not; the end of love-longings beyond understanding; the highest in all beings.
3. He is self-luminous and subtler than the smallest. In Him rest all the worlds and their beings.
4. He is the Everlasting Adam. He is life, word and mind. He is the truth and immortal life.
5. He is the shore to which we sail. He is the goal to be attained. He is the mark to be struck. Attain that mark, my beloved!
6. Take His great bow of Scriptures and place in it your arrow of devotion. Draw back the bow with your concentration on Him and hit the center of the mark, the Everlasting Spirit.
7. The bow is the wisdom of Adam; the arrow is our own soul. Adam is the mark of the arrow, the aim of our soul. Even as the arrow becomes one with the mark, let the watchful soul be one in Him.
8. Woven in Him are the sky and the earth and all the realms of the air. In Him rest the mind and the powers of life. Know Him as the One; leave

aside all other words. He is the bridge of immortality.

9. Where all the subtle channels of the body meet, where He moves in the hearts and transforms His form into many. Meditate upon Adam, your Higher Self. Glory unto you and your far-away voyage beyond darkness!

10. He who knows all and sees all and whose glory the universe shows, dwells as the Spirit and in the divine city of nine worthies called our body, and in the yet deeper realms of our heart.

11. He becomes mind and drives on the body and life. He draws power from food and finds peace in the heart. There, the wise find Him as joy, light and life eternal.

12. And when He is seen in His immanence and transcendence, ties that have bound the heart are loosened and the mind's doubts vanish.

13. In the golden chamber is Adam, indivisible and pure. He is the radiant light of all lights. This knows he who knows Adam.

14. There, the sun nor the moon nor the stars shines not. Flashes of lightning shine not, much less earthly fire. All these give light from His light. His radiance illumines all creation.

15. Far-spreading everywhere is Adam, the Spirit Eternal. In truth, Adam is all. Thou art Adam.

CHAPTER SEVENTEEN

1. TWO birds dwell on the branches of the tree of eternity. One eats the fruit thereof; the other observes in silence.
2. The first is Eve, mother of life who rests on the tree and feels sad in her ignorance. Upon seeing the power and glory of the second bird, the Spirit of Adam, she is freed from sorrow.
3. When the wise one beholds the glory of the Lord, one leaves good and evil behind and goes to the Unity Supreme.
4. In silent wonder, the wise see Him as life which flames in all creation.
5. This is the greatest seer of Adam, who, in doing all one's work does holy work, in God, in Adam, in the self; finds all one's peace and joy.
6. Adam is attained by truth and discipline, whence come wisdom and discernment. The wise who are pure and strive see him within the body in his pure and glorious light.
7. Truth obtains victory, not untruth; truth begets truth. Truth is the way that leads to the realms of light. Free from selfish desires, the wise voyage therein and reach the supreme abode of truth.
8. He is immeasurable in His light and beyond all thought, yet He shines smaller than the smallest plank.

9. Far, far away is He, yet He is near. He rests in the inmost chamber of the heart.
10. He cannot be seen by the eye; words cannot reveal Him. He cannot be reached by the senses, austerity or sacred actions.
11. By the grace, wisdom and purity of mind, he can be seen indivisible in the silence of contemplation.
12. Adam can be seen by the mind wherein the five senses are resting. All mind is woven with the senses. But in a pure mind, shines the Light of the higher self.
13. Whatever regions the pure in heart may behold within their mind; whatever desire they may have hidden in their hearts, they attain those realms and win those desires. Let the one who wishes for success give reverence to the seers of the Spirit of Adam!
14. The one knows the dwelling of Adam wherein the whole universe shines in radiance.
15. The wise who, free from selfish desire, adore the Spirit and pass beyond the seed of life in death.
16. One whose mind wanders aimlessly among desires, and is unceasingly longing for the objects of desire: how can such a one escape the strivings of life and death?
17. Verily, one such as this is enslaved by the transient. He finds appeasement in life's passing destruction.
18. But one who possesses the end of all longing and whose inner-self has found fulfillment. Even in this life, one's selfish desires will fade away like a dream when one is awoken.
19. Not through much learning is Adam reached. He is not reached through intellect or sacred

teaching. He is reached by the chosen of Him. Through the anointed He emerged His glory.
20. Adam is not reached by the weak, the careless or by those who practice vain austerity. He is reached by the wise who strive on the right course which leads the soul to the shores of Adam.
21. Having reached that supreme place, the seers find joy and wisdom. Their souls are fulfilled; their passions are and they have peace. Filled with devotion, they have found the Spirit in all and go into the All.
22. Actions and forms go to their sources and senses go to their divinities. The self and its knowledge go to the everlasting Supreme.
23. Rivers flowing into the ocean find their final peace and their name and form disappear. Likewise, the wise become free from name, form and limiting self when they enter into the radiance of the Spirit who is greater than all greatness. In truth, one who knows God becomes God. Thou art Adam.

CHAPTER EIGHTEEN

1. THIS eternal world is all: what was; what is and what shall be; what is beyond in eternity. All is Adam.
2. Adam is all. The Self is Adam. Adam, the Self, has four conditions.
3. The first condition is the waking life of outward-moving consciousness which enjoys the outer senses of life. The first state is experience.
4. The second condition is the dreaming life of inner-moving consciousness which enjoys the subtle inner elements in its own light and solitude. The second state is self-awareness.
5. The third condition is the sleeping life of the silent observer who has no desires and beholds no dreams. That condition of deep sleep is of oneness, a mass of silent consciousness made of peace and enjoying peace.
6. This silent consciousness is all-powerful and all-knowing. It is the inner ruler, the source of all, the beginning and end of all beings.
7. The fourth condition is Adam in His pure state. It is the awakened life of supreme consciousness.
8. It is neither outer nor inner awareness. It is neither quasi-awareness nor sleeping-awareness. It is neither consciousness nor unconsciousness.

9. He is Adam, the Spirit that cannot be seen or touched; the Spirit that is above all distinction, beyond all thought and inexpressible.
10. In a union with Him is the supreme proof of his reality. He is the end of evolution and non-duality. He is peace and love. Thou art Adam.

CHAPTER NINETEEN

1. THE lovers of Adam ask, "What is the source of this universe? What is Adam? From where do we come? By what power do we live? Where do we find rest? Who ruled over us, our joys and our sorrows, O seers of Adam?
2. Shall we think of time, of the nature of things, of the law of necessity, of chance, of elements, or of the power of creation of woman or of man?
3. Not a mere union of these, for above them is a soul that thinks. But our soul is under the power of pleasure and pain!
4. Through the course of meditation and contemplation, the wise saw Adam's power hidden in His own creation. It is He who rules over all sources in this universe, from time to the soul of mortals.
5. They saw the splendor of His power, the Great Whirling Wheel within wheels.
6. Rims within rims, and spokes within counter-spokes, radiant embers, and jewels of every color.
7. The geometry of every sacred degree. Paths of innumerable strands rushing into one rope. That great rainbow serpent that slithers about itself. The crashing waves of thousands of eyes which swirl about one another.

8. In the great thunderous interstellar cloud; nebula of light and love, cloud and a myriad of eyes and mouths and rims and spokes and jewels; the waters of life rushing about with senses, waves moved by breathing winds blown by the fountain of consciousness, with its dangerously violent whirlwinds of sorrows.
9. Infinite suns strung together into celestial garlands and heavenly bodies as raiment, galaxies of wafting fragrance.
10. Full of revelations; resplendent; utterly boundless and of ubiquitous regard, all gods within His heavenly body, each living thing in their degree. Universal form without limit.
11. This vast multifaceted wheel of creation, wherein all things live and die, wanders around in the soul like a beautiful swan who flies restlessly for she thinks that God is afar. But when the love of Adam comes down upon her, she finds her own immortal life that was always hers.
12. Exalted in all songs is Adam. In Him are God and the world and the soul. He is the imperishable supporter of all.
13. When the beholders of Adam grasp Him in all creation, they find peace in Him and are free from all sorrows.
14. Adam upholds the oneness of this universe: the seen and the unseen; the transient and the eternal. The soul of man is bound by pleasure and pain, but when he sees Adam, he is free from all fetters.
15. There is the soul of man with wisdom and no wisdom; power and no power. There is the soul of Mother Eve, nature, which is creation, whose sake is for the soul. And there is God—infinite,

omnipresent—who observes all of creation. When one knows all three, Thou art Adam.

16. In time, matter passes away. However, God is forever; He rules both the matter and the soul.
17. Through meditation on Him and communion with Him, there comes the destruction of earthly delusion in the end.
18. When one knows God, one is free. One's sorrows end and death is no more.
19. When in the inner-union, one is beyond the world of the body. Then the third world, the world of the Spirit, is found. Where the power of the all resides and one has all, he is one with the One.
20. Know that Adam is forever in thee; nothing higher is there to be known.
21. When one sees God, the world and the soul, one sees the three. One sees Adam.
22. Just like fire is not seen in wood, yet by the power it comes to light with fire, Adam emerges in the universe emerges and is revealed in the soul.
23. Adam is found in the soul when sought with truth and self-sacrifice just like fire is found in wood; cream in milk; the oil hidden in the fruit and the sculpture in the marble.
24. There is a spirit who is hidden in all things who is the source of self-knowledge and self-sacrifice.
25. This, in truth, is Adam. Thou art Adam.

CHAPTER TWENTY

1. ADAM—God of inspiration—sends the mind and its powers like curious ravens to find the truth. He sends the light of God's holy fire to spread over the earth.
2. By the grace of Adam, our mind is one with Him. We strive with all our power with the light.
3. Adam gives life to our souls and they shine in His great light. He makes our mind and its powers one; He leads our thoughts to the highest realms.
4. The seers of Adam who see all their minds and thoughts in oneness, sing the glory of Adam who has given every self His work.
5. I sing the song of ancient times with adoration. May my own songs follow the path of the eternal sun.
6. Let all the children of immortality hear me; even those who are in the highest heaven!
7. Where the fire of Adam burns; where the wind of the Spirit blows; where the blood-wine of God flows, a new soul is born.
8. Inspired by the Spirit, let us find joy in the prayers of the ancient times. For if we make them our rock we shall not lose our course.
9. With an upright body, head and neck, lead the mind and its powers into thy heart. The name of Adam will be thy boat with which to cross the rivers of fear.

10. And when the body is in silent steadiness, breathe rhythmically through the nostrils with a peaceful ebbing and flowing of breath. The ship of the mind is tossed about by unsteady winds; those wild winds of the mind must be tamed.
11. Find a tranquil retreat for the practice of mental discipline. One that is sheltered from the elements; clean and level; free from debris and ugliness; where the sound of the waters and the beauty of the scenery aid in thoughtful contemplation.
12. These are such visions that precede a final embrace of Adam in the mind: mists, smoke, suns, winds, fireflies, sparks, flashes of lightning, crystals, fractals, moons and gemstones.
13. When the wise have complete power over their body, they obtain a new body of spiritual fire which does not get sick, age or die.
14. The first fruits of this practice are manifested properly when one eats a diet of animals.
15. The meal of plants, nuts and seeds is not a proper meal for us. A burning of plants and logs for fuel is poison for man's body. A diet of animals for sustenance is a higher path. But respect for the Spirit within the sacrifice is still the highest path.
16. Indeed, plants are a medicinal and should not be shunned. All things have a proper place: animals for food; plants for medicine; truffles, stalks and caps for the Spirit. Consider the lily, toiling not, blue with heavenly bliss.
17. Meat is good for our body and soul alike. Also, insects and fungi and every manner of creeping thing. Likewise, eggs, and butter, and cheeses, and fats, and jerky and pemmican; livers and all manner of organs.

18. Let the skins be peeled, and worn as clothing, Lord Adam's provision to keep upward and dry.
19. Let the milk comfort the bellies of children, and of those with poor countenance. Let the cream froth, and fill bellies at the celebrations.
20. Praise be to Adam for becoming the Spirit of the cattle, and for becoming the sacrifice for our conquest of wisdom. Thou Art Adam.

CHAPTER TWENTY-ONE

1. A gold mirror covered by dust shines in full splendor when cleaned and polished. When one has seen the truth of the Spirit and is one with Him, the aim of life is fulfilled; one is every beyond sorrow.
2. One's soul becomes a lamp with which one finds the truth of Adam.
3. One sees God—pure, never-born and everlasting—and is freed from all bondage.
4. This is the God whose light illumines all creation; the Creator of all. He was; He is; He forever shall be. He is all. He sees all.
5. Glory be to the God who is in all things in this vast creation. Unto that Spirit be glory!
6. There is One in whose hands is the net of Eve, illusion. With His power, He rules all the worlds.
7. He is the same at the time of creation and at the time of dissolution. Those who know Him attain immortality.
8. He is Adam. He governs the worlds with His power. He watches over all; He rules over their creation and their destruction.
9. His eyes and mouth are everywhere; His arms and feet are in all places. He is God who made the heaven and the earth and all things in it.

10. May Adam—the seer of eternity who gave the gods their birth and their glory; who keeps all things under his protection; who, in the beginning, created the Golden Seed—grant us the grace of pure vision.
11. Come down to us, Spirit who art in the high mountains. Come, let the light of Thy face which is free from fear and evil, shine upon us. Come to us with Thy love.
12. Greater than all is Adam—the Supreme, the Infinite, the Sovereign. He dwells in the mystery of all beings who dwell according to their form in nature.
13. Those who know Him know all, and in those whose glory all things are, attain immortality.
14. I know the Spirit, radiant like the sun beyond darkness. He who knows him goes beyond death, for He is the only path to life immortal.
15. His infinity is beyond what is great or small. Greater than Him there is nothing.
16. Like an everlasting tree, He stands in the center of heaven. His radiance illumines all creation.
17. Those who know Him who is greater than all and is beyond form and pain, attain immortality. Those who know Him not, go to self-created worlds of unending sorrow.
18. This universe is in the glory of God, the Spirit of love. The heads and faces of all are His own, and He is in the hearts of all.
19. He is indeed the Lord whose grace moves the hearts of men. He leads them unto His own joy and to the glory of His light.
20. He is the inmost soul of all which is like a little flame the size of a teardrop that is hidden in the hearts of men.

21. He is the master of wisdom reached through thought and love. He is the immortality of those who know Him.
22. He has innumerable heads and eyes and feet. His vastness enfolds the universe.
23. God is in truth, the whole universe. He is what was, what is and what shall be. He is the God of all life.
24. His hands and feet are everywhere. He has heads and mouths everywhere. He sees all; He hears all. He is in all. He is all.
25. The light of consciousness comes to Him through infinite powers of emergent perception. Yet, He is above these powers. He is God—the ruler of all and the infinite refuge of all.
26. Without hands, He holds all things. Without feet, he runs everywhere. Without eyes, He sees all things. Without ears, He hears all things. He knows all, but no-one knows Him.
27. Concealed in the heart of all beings is Adam who is smaller than the smallest atom and greater than the greatest spaces. When one sees God's glory, by his grace, one sees Him beyond the world of desire and all sorrows are left behind.
28. I know the Spirit whose infinity is in all; He is ever one beyond time. I know the Spirit whom the lovers of Adam call eternal. Thou art Adam.

CHAPTER TWENTY-TWO

1. MAY God who, in the mystery of His vision and power, transforms into his many-faceted creation from whom all things come and into whom they all return, grant us the grace of pure vision.
2. He is the sun, the moon and the stars. He is the fire, the waters and the wind. He is Adam, the Lord of all of his creation.
3. Thou art this boy, and thou art this maiden. Thou art this man, and thou art this woman. Thou art this old man who supports himself on a staff. Thou art God who appears in infinite forms.
4. Thou the bluebird, and thou the blackbird. Thou the cloud that conceals the lightning. Thou the seasons and the oceans. Beyond beginning, thou art thy infinity, and all the worlds had their beginning in thee.
5. There is nature, never-born Mother Eve who—with light, fire and darkness—creates all things in nature. There is the never-born soul of man bound by the pleasures of Mother Eve. There is the Spirit of Adam who has left behind the pleasures in the joy of the beyond.
6. Two birds dwell among the branches of the tree of eternity. The one is obliviously immersed and eats the fruit thereof. The second perceives in silence.
7. The first is the natural self who rests on the tree while feeling sad in her ignorance. Upon

beholding the power and glory of the higher Spirit, she is freed from all sorrow.

8. Of what use are the Scriptures to one who does not know the Spirit from which they come, and in whom all things abide?
9. For only those who have found Him have found peace.
10. For all things come from the Spirit. With Eve, His power of mystery and wonder, He made all things. By Eve, the human soul is bound.
11. Know that Mother Eve, nature is an illusion, but that Adam is the ruler of nature. All beings in the universe are parts of His infinite splendor.
12. He rules over the sources of creation. From Him comes the universe; unto Him, it returns. He is the Lord—the giver of blessings and the God of adoration—in whom there is perfect peace.
13. May Adam—the seer of Eternity who gave to all men and gods their birth and glory; who keeps all things under His protection; who saw the Golden Seed in the beginning—grant us His grace of pure vision.
14. Who is the God to whom we shall offer adoration? The God of gods in whose glory the worlds are; the one who rules this universe.
15. He is the God of infinite forms in whose glory all things are, smaller than the smallest length of a planck, yet the Creator of all, ever-living in the mystery, the memory of His creation. In the vision of this God of love, there is everlasting peace.
16. He is the Lord of all who, hidden in the heart of things, watches over the world. The gods and the seers of Adam are one with him. When one knows Him, one cuts the bonds of death.

17. When one knows God in whose glory all things are, one is free from all bondage.
18. This is the God whose work is all the worlds. He is the Supreme Soul who dwells forever in the hearts of men. Those who know Him through their hearts and their minds become immortal.
19. There is a region beyond darkness where there is neither day nor night nor what is nor what is not. There is only Adam, the God of love. It is the region of the glorious splendor of God from whom came the light of the sun and the ancient wisdom.
20. The mind cannot grasp Him above, below or in the space between. With whom shall we compare Him whose glory is the whole universe?
21. Far beyond the range of vision, He cannot be seen by natural eyes. However, He can be known by the heart and the mind. Those who know Him attain immortality.
22. O Lord, Such a one comes to Thee in fearful wonder and says, "Thou art God who never was born. Let thy face, O Adam, shine upon me. Let Thy love be my eternal protection.
23. Hold fast my child and the child of my child. Hold fast my life. Hold fast our brave men for we ever come to Thee in adoration. Thou art Adam."

CHAPTER TWENTY-THREE

1. TWO things are hidden in the mystery of the infinity of Adam: knowledge and ignorance. Ignorance passes away and knowledge is immortal. Adam is in eternity above ignorance and knowledge.
2. He is the One in whose power are the sources of creation; the root and the flower of all things. The Golden Seed—the Creator—was in His mind in the beginning; He saw Him born when time began.
3. He is God who casts the net of transmigration and then withdraws it in the sea of life. He is the Lord who created the lords of creation. He is the Supreme Soul who rules over all.
4. Even as the sun shines everywhere above the clouds, so does the glory of God rule over all creation.
5. In the unfolding of His own nature, He makes all things blossom into flower and fruit. He gives them all their fragrance and color. He is the One. He is the only God who rules the universe.
6. There is a spirit hidden in the mystery of the Scriptures. Adam, the God of Creation, owns it as his own creator. It is the Spirit of God. It is seen by the gods and seers of ancient times who, when one with Him, became immortal.

7. When one is bound by the selfish power of nature, one works only for selfish rewards. In time, one has their reward.
8. The soul is like a sun in splendor. When it becomes one with the self-conscious "I am" and its desires, it is the flame the size of a teardrop. When it is one with pure reason and the inner Spirit, it becomes in concentration as the point of a needle.
9. The soul can be thought of as the part of a point of a hair which divided by a hundred were divided a hundred again. Yet in this living soul, there is the seed of infinity.
10. The soul is not a man nor a woman. It is born and unfolds in a body with dreams and desires for the meat of life. The Spirit of Adam is then reborn in new bodies with new dreams, desires and hunger.
11. The quality of souls and experiences vary in accordance with the wisdom gained. But all is experienced and remembered by Adam.
12. There is the God of forms infinite. When one knows God, he is free from all bondage. He is the Creator of all who is ever-living in the mystery of His creation. He is beyond the beginning and end. In his glorious mind, all things are.
13. He is the incorporeal Spirit, and He can be seen by a heart which is pure. Beings and non-beings spring forth from Him; He is the Creator of all. He is Adam, the God of love. When one knows Him, one leaves behind all sorrows and transmigrates into the bosom of the Spirit. Thou art Adam.

CHAPTER TWENTY-FOUR

1. SOME saints speak of the nature of things as the cause of the world. Others, in their delusion, speak of time. It is by the glory of God that the great multifaceted wheel of Adam revolves in the universe.
2. The whole universe is ever in His power. He is pure consciousness and the Creator of time. He is all-powerful and all-knowing. He is all strength and all meaning.
3. It is under His rule that the work of creation revolves in its evolution, and we have earth, water, fire, air, life and spirit.
4. God ended His work and He rested. He made a bond of love between his soul and the soul of all things. The One became one with the one, and the two, and the three, and the eight, and with time and subtle mystery, of the human soul.
5. His first works are bound by the confines of nature to the place given to each role. When nature is overcome, the work is done, and a greater work can begin.
6. His being is the source of all beings. It is the seed of all things that, in this life, have their lives.
7. He is beyond time and space. Yet he is the God of forms infinite who dwells in our inmost thoughts, and who is seen by those who love Him.

The Testament of Adam

8. He is beyond the tree of life, time and things seen by mortal eyes. The whole universe comes from Him.
9. He gives us the truth and takes away evil, for He is the Lord of all good.
10. Know that He is the inmost of thy soul and that He is the home of thy immortality.
11. May we know the Lord of lords, the King of kings, the God of gods, the God of love and Lord of all.
12. We cannot see how He grows the world, nor what are the tools of His cultivation. Nothing can be compared with Him; how can anything be greater than He is? His power is shown in infinite ways. How great are His works and wisdom!
13. No one was ever before He was. No one has rule over Him. He is the source and ruler of all.
14. May God who is hidden in nature, like a silkworm is hidden in the web of silk she made, lead us to union with His own Spirit, with Adam.
15. He is God, hidden in all beings, their inmost soul who is in all. He watches the works of creation. He lives in all things and watches over them.
16. He is pure consciousness. He is beyond the conditions of nature. He rules the work of silence of many. He transforms one seed into many. Only those who see God in their soul attain eternal joy.
17. He is the eternal among things that pass away. He fulfills the prayers of many. By the vision of Adam, one knows God. When one knows God, one is freed from all fetters.
18. There, where the sun nor the moon nor the stars shine not. Flashes of lightning shine not, much less earthly fire. All these give light from His light; His radiance illumines all creation.

19. He is the wandering swan. He is the soul of all in the universe. He is the Spirit of fire in the ocean of life. To know Him is to overcome death, and He is the only course of eternal life.
20. He is the never-created Creator of all. He knows all. He is pure consciousness. He is the all-powerful and all-knowing Creator of time.
21. He is the Lord of the soul, of nature and of the conditions of nature. From Him comes the transmigration of life and liberation; bondage in time and freedom in eternity.
22. He is the God of light and loving protector of all. He is immortal in His glory. He is the everlasting ruler of the word. Could there be any other ruler but Him?
23. Longing for liberation, I seek refuge in God who reveals His light by His grace. I seek refuge in The Spirit of Adam who created the god of creation and gave to him the sacred word.
24. I seek refuge in God who is one in the silence of eternity, pure radiance of beauty and perfection. In Him we find peace.
25. He is the bridge which leads to immortality. He is the fire which burns away the chaff of lower life.
26. If ever it was possible for one to fold the tent of the sky, one might also be able to end his sorrow without God's help.
27. By the power of inner harmony and by the grace of God, Thou art Adam.

CHAPTER TWENTY-FIVE

1. THIS is the knowledge of Adam, as found hidden in all the Scriptures and as revealed by Saint Adam.
2. The Spirit is among the things of this world. He is also above the things of this world. He is clear, pure and in the peace of a void of vastness.
3. He is beyond the life of the body and the mind. He was never born, and He will never die. He is one in His own greatness.
4. He is the Spirit whose power gives consciousness to the body. He is the Captain of the vessel.
5. When one is asleep, he does not know if he will wake up. Likewise, part of the subtle Spirit comes as an angel to the body without the body being conscious of its arrival.
6. A part of the infinite consciousness becomes our own finite consciousness with powers of discrimination and definition, and with false conceptions. Adam is the truth. He is the source of creation and the universe within us all.
7. This Spirit is consciousness and gives consciousness to the body. He is the Captain of the vessel.
8. The poets of ancient times say this is the Spirit who wanders on this earth from body to body, free

from the light and darkness which follows our works.

9. He is free because He is free from selfishness. He is invisible, incomprehensible and hidden in darkness. He seems to work and to not be, but in truth, He works not, and He is.

10. He is His own being. He watches the drama of the universe.

11. He is hidden behind the veil of nature and the universe. In the joy of his law of righteousness, He is ever one.

12. The soul rules the body, but the immortal soul is pure like a drop of water. The human soul is under the power of nature, and thus it falls into confusion.

13. Because of this confusion, the soul cannot become conscious of the God who dwells within and whose power enables us to work.

14. The soul is whirled along the rushing stream of muddy waters of nature. It becomes unsteady and is filled with confusion. It is filled with desires and pride.

15. Whenever the soul has thoughts of "I" and "mine," it binds itself with its lower self.

16. "Adam is," thus says the beholder of Adam.

17. "Adam is the door," thus speaks one of austere harmony whose sins have been washed away.

18. "Everything is the glory of Adam," says the saint who is forever meditating on Adam.

19. Therefore, it is through vision, harmony and contemplation that Adam is attained.

20. In the beginning, all was Adam. His infinity is everywhere.

21. In Him, there is neither above nor across nor below. In Him, there is neither east nor west nor past nor future.
22. The Spirit is immeasurable, inapprehensible, beyond conception, never-born, beyond reasoning and beyond thought. His vastness is the vastness of space.
23. At the end of the worlds, all things sleep. He alone is awake in eternity.
24. From His infinite space, new worlds arise, a universe which is a vastness of thought.
25. In the consciousness of Adam, the universe is expanded; into Him, it returns.
26. He is seen in the radiance of the sun in the sky, in the brightness of the fire on the earth and in the fire of life that burns the meat of life.
27. He who is in the sun, in the fire and in the heart of man is one. He who knows this is one with the One.
28. When the wise one has mentally withdrawn from all things without; when one's spirit of life has peacefully left inner sensations, let him rest in peace as he is freed from the movements of will and desire.
29. Since the living being called the Spirit of life has come from that which is greater than the spirit of life, let the spirit of life surrender itself into that fourth condition of consciousness which is greater than the spirit of life.
30. There is something beyond our mind which abides in silence within our mind. It is the mystery beyond thought. Let one's mind and inner self rest on that.

31. There are two ways to contemplate on Adam: through sound and silence. By sound, we go to silence.
32. The sound of Adam is utterance. With utterance, we go to the end: the silence of Adam. The end is immortality, union and peace.
33. Even as a spider reaches the liberty of space with its own thread, the man of contemplation reaches freedom through utterance.
34. The sound of Adam is utterance. At the end of the utterance, there is silence. It is a joyful silence.
35. It is the end of the journey where fear and sorrow are no more: steady, motionless, never falling, everlasting and immortal. It is called the omnipresent Adam.
36. In order to reach the Highest, meditate on the sound and silence of Adam.
37. For it had been said that God is the sound and silence. His name is Adam. Therefore, contemplate on silence in Him.
38. Fire without fuel finds its peace in its resting place. Likewise, when thoughts become silence, the soul finds peace in its own source.
39. And when a mind which longs for truth finds the peace of its own source, false inclinations, which were a result of actions done under the delusions of the senses, cease.
40. Transcendence, rapturous quickening and the transmigration of life, take place in one's own mind. Therefore, let one keep the mind pure. What one thinks, one becomes.
41. A quietness of mind overcomes good and evil works. In quietness, the soul is one.
42. If men thought of God as much as they think of the world, who would not attain liberation?

43. The mind pure when free from desire. It is impure when in the bondage of desire.
44. When the mind is silent, beyond weakness or non-concentration, it can enter into a world which is far beyond the mind; the highest end.
45. The mind should be kept in the heart as long as it has not reached the highest end. This is wisdom and liberation. Everything else is only worlds.
46. Words cannot describe the joy of a soul whose impurities are cleansed and is one with Adam. Only those who feel this joy know what it is.
47. Just like water becomes one with water; fire with fire and air with air, the mind becomes one with the infinite mind and attains final freedom.
48. The mind is the source of both bondage and liberation. To be bound to the things of this world is bondage. To be free of them is liberation.
49. Glory be to Adam—the God of fire—who dwells in the earth and remembers the world. Give this world unto those that adore Thee!
50. Glory be to Adam—the God of the wind—who dwells in the air and remembers this world. Give this world to those who adore Thee!
51. Glory be to Adam—the God of the sun—who dwells in the heavens and remembers this world. Give this world to them that adore Thee!
52. Glory be to Adam—the sun—who dwells in the sky. Give this world to those who adore Thee, Lord! Thou art Adam.

CHAPTER TWENTY-SIX

1. WHEN one is speaking, one cannot be breathing; this is the sacrifice of breath for speech. And when one is breathing, one cannot be speaking; this is the sacrifice of speech for breath.
2. These are the two never-ending immortal offerings of man, whether one is awake or asleep.
3. These are the three adorations of the saint:
4. At the rising sun, the saint said, "You who give freedom, make me free."
5. When the sun was mid-way in heaven, the saint said, "You who are on high and give freedom, set me on high and make me free."
6. At the hour of sunset, he uttered this prayer, "You who give full freedom, make me fully free."
7. When the fire burns, Adam shines. When the fire dies, Adam goes. Its light goes to the sun. Its breath of life goes to the wind.
8. When the sun shines, Adam shines. When the sun sets, Adam goes. Its light goes to the moon. Its breath goes to the wind.
9. When the moon shines, Adam shines. When the moon sets, Adam goes. Its light goes to a flash of lightning. Its breath of life goes to the wind.
10. When a flash of lightning shines, Adam shines. When it goes, Adam goes. Its light goes to the

regions of heaven. Its breath of life goes to the wind.

11. A great and devoted saint who loved Adam and fought the inner fight with all his soul reached the dwelling of the love of God.
12. Adam spoke unto the saint. "Beloved, ask for a gift." To this, the saint replied, "I ask for that gift which You think is best for mankind."
13. "A master imposes not a gift upon his pupil" said Adam. "Ask for any gift you like."
14. "Then I shall not have a gift," determined the saint.
15. Adam said to His devotee, "Know Me for this is the best for man."
16. "I am the breath of life. I am the consciousness of life. Adore Me. Think of Me as life and immortality."
17. "The breath of life is one. When we speak, life speaks. When we see, life sees. When we hear, life hears. When we think, life thinks. When we breathe, life breathes."
18. "And there is something greater than the breath of life. One can live without speech; we can see the dumb.
19. "One can live without sight; we can see the blind. One can live without hearing; we can see the deaf. One can live without a right mind; we can see those who are mad."
20. "But it is consciousness of life which becomes the breath of life and gives life to a body. The breath of life is the consciousness of life, and the consciousness of life is the breath of life."
21. "When consciousness rules speech, we can speak all words."

22. "When consciousness rules breath, we can smell all perfumes."
23. When consciousness rules the eye, we can see all forms.
24. When consciousness rules the ear, we can hear all sounds.
25. When consciousness rules the tongue, we can savor all tastes.
26. When the consciousness rules the mind, we can think all thoughts.
27. It is not speech which we ought to want to know. We ought to want to know the speaker.
28. It is not things seen which we ought to want to know. We ought to know the seer.
29. It is not the sound which we ought to want to know. We ought to know the hearer.
30. It is not the mind which we ought to want to know. We should know the thinker. Thou art Adam.

CHAPTER TWENTY-SEVEN

1. I will speak words of truth. The divine law shall be on my lips. May the sacred knowledge illumine us. May we attain the glory of wisdom.
2. Lord, let me come unto Thee. Come thou unto me, O Lord. In Thy waters, O my Lord, may I wash my sins away.
3. What is needful? Righteousness, sacred learning and teaching. Truth, sacred learning and teaching. Meditation, sacred learning and teaching. Self-control, sacred learning and teaching. Ritual, sacred learning and teaching. Peace, sacred learning and teaching. Humanity, sacred learning and teaching.
4. The truthful says "truth." The austere say "austerity." But one who is beyond pleasure and pain says, "Learning and teaching."
5. He who knows Adam—who is truth, consciousness and infinite joy; who is hidden in the inmost of our soul and in the highest heaven—enjoys all things he desires in communion with the all-knowing Adam.
6. In the beginning, space came from Adam. From space came air; from the air, fire. From fire came water. From the water came solid earth. From solid earth came living plants. From plants came seed and meat. From seed and meat came self-aware mankind; from mankind, Adam.

7. Whoever denies God denies Himself. Whoever affirms God affirms Himself.
8. Joy comes from God. Who could live or breathe if the joy of Adam filled not the universe?
9. If one places a gulf between himself and God, this gulf will bring fear. But if one finds the support of the invisible and ineffable, one is free from fear.
10. Words and mind go to Him. They reach Him not and return. But he who knows the joy of Adam, fears no more.
11. Once, a voyager who was devoted to Adam's truth said, "Father, explain to me the inner mystery of Adam."
12. Then the wise man bearing stalk and cap came to him. He said, "Seek to know Him from whom all beings come, by whom they all live and unto whom they return. He is Adam."
13. So the seeker went and practiced discipline and prayer. He thought Adam was the food of the earth for from the earth, all beings have come. Through the food of the earth, they all live. Unto the earth, they all return.
14. After this, he humbly returned to the wise one. "Father, explain further to me the mystery of Adam," he requested. To this, the seer answered, "Seek to know Adam through meditation and prayer because Adam is prayer."
15. The seeker went and practiced disciplined meditation and spiritual prayer. He thought that Adam was life for from life, all beings have come. Through life, they all live. Unto life, they all return.
16. After this, he returned to the prophet. "Kin of my eternal clan, explain to me the mystery of Adam," he requested. To this, the wise one replied, "Seek

to know Adam through spiritual prayer for Adam is prayer."
17. So, the seeker practiced disciplined spiritual prayer. He thought that Adam was mind for from the mind, all beings have come. Through the mind, they all live. Unto the mind, they all return.
18. And he went again to the teacher. He pleaded, "Father, explain to me the mystery of Adam." To this, the wise one answered, "Seek to know Adam through spiritual prayer because Adam is prayer."
19. So the seeker went and performed spiritual prayer. He thought Adam was reason because from reason, all beings have come. Through reason, they all live. Unto reason, they all return.
20. He returned again to the wise one. He requested the same information and received the same answer.
21. So he went and practiced meditation and spiritual prayer. He saw that Adam is joy because from joy, all beings have come. Through joy, all beings live. Unto joy, all beings return.
22. "Oh, the wonder of joy! I am the food of life. I am He who eats the food of life. I am the two in one. I am the first-born of the domain of truth; born before the gods; born in the center of immortality.
23. He who gives me is my salvation. I am the food which eats the eater of the food. I have gone beyond the universe. The light of the sun is my light."

Thou art Adam.

CHAPTER TWENTY-EIGHT

1. WHEREFORE do all these worlds come? They come from space. All beings arise from space; into space, they return. Indeed, space is their beginning; it is their final end.
2. Adam, the Creator of all, rested in life-giving meditations over the worlds of His creation. From them, came utterance. From utterance, came three words: earth, air and sky.
3. From these words, came all words. From those words, came speech. Just like leaves come from a stem, speech comes from words. Utterance is the whole universe.
4. Great is the most sacred sound of the holy Scriptures. But, how much greater is the infinity of Adam? A quarter of His being is the whole vast universe; the other three quarters are his heaven of immortality.
5. There is a light that shines beyond the heavens and all things on earth. This is the light that shines in our heart.
6. This universe is Adam. He is the beginning, the end and the life of all. In silence, bestow adoration upon Him.
7. One in truth is made of faith. As one's faith is in this life, so one becomes in the beyond: with faith and vision let one work.

8. There is a Spirit that is mind and life, light and truth and vast spaces. He contains all works, desires, perfumes and tastes. He enfolds the whole universe; He is loving to all.
9. This is the Spirit that is in my heart; it is smaller than a grain of rice.
10. This is the Spirit that is in my heart; it greater than the earth or the sky. It is greater than heaven itself.
11. He contains all works, desires, perfumes and tastes. He enfolds the whole universe; He is loving to all. This is the Spirit that is in my heart. This is Adam.
12. To Him, I shall come when I go beyond this life. And to Him, will come one who has faith and doubts not. Thou art Adam.
13. I go to the imperishable treasure. By His grace; by His grace; by His grace.
14. I go to the Spirit of life. By His grace; by His grace; by His grace.
15. I go to the Spirit of the earth. By His grace; by His grace; by His grace.
16. I go to the Spirit of the air. By His grace; by His grace; by His grace.
17. I go to the Spirit of the heavens. By His grace; by His grace; by His grace.
18. We should consider that in the inner world, Adam is consciousness. We should consider that in the outer world, He is space. These are the two meditations.
19. The invisible and subtle essence is the Spirit of the whole universe. That is reality. That is truth. Thou art God.
20. Is there anything higher than thought? Meditation is, in truth, higher than thought. The

earth seems to rest in silent meditation. The waters, the mountains, the sky and the heavens all seem to be in meditation. Whenever one attains greatness on this earth, he has his reward according to his meditation.

21. When one speaks words of truth, he speaks words of greatness. Know the nature of truth.
22. When one knows, one can speak the truth. Know the nature of knowledge.
23. When one thinks, one can know. One who does not think does not know. Know the nature of thought.
24. When one has faith, one thinks. One who has no faith does not think. Know the nature of faith.
25. Where there is progress, one sees and has faith. Where there is no progress, there is no faith. Know the nature of progress.
26. When there is creation, there is progress. When there is no creation, there is no progress. Know the nature of creation.
27. Where there is joy, there is creation. Where there is no joy, there is no creation. Know the nature of joy.
28. Where there is the Infinite, there is joy. Where there is no Infinite, there is no joy. Know the nature of the Infinite.
29. Where nothing else is seen, heard or known, there is the Infinite. Where something is seen, heard or known, there is the finite. The Infinite is immortal. The finite is mortal.
30. "Where does the Infinite rest?" On His own greatness or not even on His own greatness.
31. In this world, they call greatness the possession of many recourses, lands, women and houses. But I do not call this greatness for here, one thing depends upon another.

32. But the Infinite is everywhere. It is the whole universe.
33. I am everywhere. I am the whole Universe.
34. Adam is everywhere. He is the whole universe.
35. One who sees, knows, and understands this, who finds in Adam, the Spirit, His love and His pleasure and His union and His joy, becomes a Master of oneself. One's freedom is infinite.
36. But those who do not see this become the servants of other masters. In the worlds that pass away, they attain not their liberation.

CHAPTER TWENTY-NINE

1. IN the center of Adam's castle, our own body, there is a small shrine in the form of a rose. Within it, is a small space. We should find who dwells there. We should want to know Him.
2. If anyone asks, "Who is He who dwells in a small shrine in the center of Adam's castle? Who should we want to find and know?" we can say this:
3. "The little space within the heart is a great as the vast universe. The heavens and the earth are there. The whole universe is in Him and He dwells within our heart."
4. And if they should ask, "If the things are in the castle of Adam, what remains when old age overcomes the castle or when the body is lifeless?" we can say this:
5. "The Spirit, who is in the body, does not grow old and does not die. No one can ever kill the Spirit who is everlasting. This is the real Adam's castle where dwells the love of the universe.
6. It is Adam, the pure Spirit that does not age or die. It is Adam whose love is truth and whose thoughts are truth.
7. As a king's entourage obeys him and follows him wherever he goes, so all love which is truth and all thoughts of truth obey Adam.
8. There is a bridge between time and eternity. This bridge is Adam.

9. Evil or sin cannot cross that bridge, because the world of the Spirit is pure. This is why when this bridge is crossed, the blind can see; the wounded are healed and the lame man becomes whole.
10. To the one who goes over that bridge, the night becomes like day. In the worlds of the Spirit, there is a light which is everlasting.
11. There is a Spirit which is pure and is beyond old age and death.
12. This is Adam, the Spirit of man. All the desires of this Spirit are truth. It is this Spirit that we must find and know. One who has found and knows one's own soul has found all the worlds and achieved all desires.
13. Know that when the eye looks into space, it is the Spirit of man that sees. The eye is only the organ of sight.
14. When one says, "I smell this perfume," it is the Spirit that feels. He uses the organ to smell.
15. When one says, "I am speaking," it is the Spirit that speaks. The voice is an organ for speech.
16. When one says, "I am hearing," it is the Spirit that hears. The ear is an organ for hearing.
17. And when one says, "I can think," it is the Spirit that thinks. The mind is the organ for thinking. It is because of the light of the Spirit that the human mind can see, think and enjoy this world.
18. All the gods in the heaven adore the contemplation of their infinite, supreme Spirit. This is why they have all joy, all the worlds and all desires. And the one who finds and knows Adam, has all his holy desires, worlds and joy. Thou art Adam.

CHAPTER THIRTY

1. LORD Adam, lead me from delusion to truth. Lead me from darkness to light. Lead me from death to immortality. Thou art Adam.
2. This universe is a trinity made of name, form and action.
3. The source of all names is the word. It is by the word that all names are spoken.
4. The word is behind all names, and Adam is behind the word.
5. The source of all forms is the eye. It is by the eye that all forms are seen. The eye is behind all forms, and Adam is behind the eye.
6. The source of all actions is the body. It is by the body that all actions are done. The body is behind all actions, and Adam is behind the body.
7. Those three are one. They are Adam, and Adam is those three.
8. The Spirit of life is the immortal. Name and form are the real. Through them, the Spirit is veiled. Thou art Adam.
9. There was once a great seer Michael, a wiseard, who was profound in knowledge and abounding in love for Adam.
10. He listened to the guidance of the Spirit with every action. He meditated in prayer to the Highest with every thought.

11. Though renowned by the world over and recognized by him was the status called equal without robbery to kings and kings of kings, he thought it nothing of him to keep reputation by wealth and hordes of treasure but took upon the nomadic mantle of counselor and friend of many.
12. At times, Michael could be found at the manors of Lords and Chieftains. He often resided in towns and stables. He drank with the common-folk, sailors and war-hardened veterans.
13. At a certain time, he found himself in the presence of King David I, who had heard of his great wisdom and sought knowledge.
14. "I will give you a thousand gifts if you can teach me the ways of God."
15. Michael sat down on the ground. He momentarily narrowed one of his eyes at the king. Then he closed his eye for a long time in contemplation.
16. He asked the Spirit of life for guidance on what his actions should be. He waited expectantly.
17. A wash of light came over his being. He smiled blissfully and said, "I, who have sacrificed more than you ever will for knowledge.
18. "I know that I hung on a wind-rocked tree, nine whole nights, with a spear wounded, and to Adam offered, myself to myself; on that tree, of which no one knows from what root it springs. I am willing to teach you about Adam."
19. Furthermore, he said, "You must portion a gift to me. A tenth of your kingdom must become mine."
20. The king pondered and resolved that his path to holy honor was worth any lavishness. He said, "Agreed. As long as the wealth of my kingdom stays undivided and whole.

21. You must reside with me and be a light unto my entire kingdom for as long as we are in darkness."
22. This allegiance was to spark a long and plentiful kinship.
23. Michael began, "There is a spirit in the sun. I adore that spirit as Adam."
24. "How can you say that?" replied David. "For I only considered the sun as the ruler of radiance and the source of all beings on earth."
25. Then Michael said, "There is a spirit in the moon far away. I adore that spirit as Adam."
26. The king answered, "I only considered the moon as the ruler of the sacred water whose waves are clothed in whiteness."
27. "There is a spirit in lightning," said the wise one, "and I adore that spirit as Adam."
28. "I only considered lightning," said the king, "as a thing of brightness."
29. The saint said, "There is a spirit in the ethereal places, and I adore that spirit as Adam."
30. "How can you say that?" replied the king. "I only considered the ethereal places as non-evolving fullness."
31. Michael spoke, "There is a spirit in the wind. I adore that spirit as Adam."
32. "I only considered the winds as an unconquerable army," answered David.
33. Michael said, "There is a great spirit in fire. I adore that spirit as Adam."
34. "I only considered fire as great power," said the king.
35. "There is a spirit in water," the wise one said, "and I adore that spirit as Adam."
36. The king answered, "I only considered water as a beautiful reflection."

37. "There is a spirit in a mirror, and I adore that spirit as Adam," said Michael.
38. "I only consider a mirror as something brilliant," David responded.
39. The master said, "There is a spirit in the sound of the steps of a man. I adore that spirit as Adam."
40. "How can you say that?" cried David. "I only considered that sound as a sign of life."
41. Michael said, "There is a spirit in the angels of heaven. I adore that spirit as Adam."
42. "I only considered the angels of heaven as companions who are ever with us," the king said.
43. There is a spirit which is a shadow," said the wiseard, "and I adore that spirit as Adam."
44. "How can you say that?" said the seeker of wisdom. "I only considered this shadow as death."
45. The saint said, "There is a spirit in the human body, and I adore that spirit as Adam."
46. "I only considered the body as the covering of a soul," replied the king.
47. And Michael fell back into a trance. With his eyes closed, his muscles twitched though not violently.
48. David called him by name, but he did not wake up.
49. The king grabbed his hand and shook him. Michael woke up. "When I was gone, where was my consciousness? And when I awoke, wherefrom did it return?" But the pupil did not know the answer.
50. "When a man is asleep, his soul takes the consciousness of the senses. The soul goes to rest with them in the Spirit who is in the human heart.
51. When all the senses are quiet, the man is said to be asleep. Then the soul holds the powers of life—mouth, eye, ear and mind—and they rest in the quietness.

52. When the soul is in the land of dreams, it dimly peers through the portal at the infinite consciousness. All the worlds then belong to the soul. One can be a great king or even a god and live in high or low conditions.
53. A great king of this earth takes his attendants with him and goes about his dominions wherever he desires. Likewise, the soul of one takes the powers of life and wanders in the land of dreams according to one's desires.
54. When one sleeps in the deep meditation of the Adam slumber, and all consciousness is gone through the infinite little channels which lead to the center of the heart from its circumference, the soul rests in the covering around the heart.
55. Just like a prince, a king or a great god finds peace or fullness of joy, the soul of one has now found peace.
56. Just like airy threads come from a spider or small sparks come from a fire, from Adam, comes all the powers of life, all the worlds and all the gods.
57. To know Adam is to know the mystery of the universe: the truth of truth. The powers of life and their truth are Adam. Thou art Adam."
58. After hearing all the words of the great wiseard Michael, King David fell down and kissed his feet. Then the eyes of his heart were opened.
59. In loving kindness towards this great and wonderful teacher, King David fulfilled his promise. He gave a tenth of his kingdom to Michael.
60. Because he was a wise and cunning ruler, he also gave his daughter Sophia to him in marriage. This sealed a permanent alliance and allegiance to the saint.

61. Michael accepted his bounty and Sophia's hand in marriage. This was not because of any temptation or desire to depart his ascetic course; the Spirit distinctly prompted him to sail that course.
62. The king said to Michael, "I hereby put you in charge of the whole kingdom." He took his signet ring from his finger and put it on Michael's finger.
63. The king dressed him in robes of fine linen and put a gold chain around his neck. He had him as his second-in-command and in charge of the whole land.
64. Then David said to Michael, "I am King, but without your word, no one will lift hand or foot in all the kingdom." David gave Michael the title Arch-Wiseard and gave him his wife.
65. And Michael went out from the king's presence and traveled throughout the far lands. He took many wives and sired many blood kin. He also made many improvements to the kingdom.
66. For many years after that, Michael instructed King David as a trusted advisor. Many a war they fought together, and victory was theirs. Thou art Adam.

CHAPTER THIRTY-ONE

1. "SOPHIA," Michael spoke unto his wife. "I am going to leave this present life and retire to a life of meditation. Let me settle my possessions upon you and your father."
2. "If all the earth filled with riches belonged to me, O Lord," said Sophia, "should I thereby attain eternal life?"
3. "Certainly not," said the saint. "Your life would only be as the life of wealthy people. In wealth, there is no hope of eternal life."
4. Sophia cried, "What should I do with possessions that cannot give me eternal life? Give me instead, your knowledge, O my Lord."
5. On hearing this, Michael exclaimed, "Dear you are to me beloved, and dear are the words you say. Come, sit down and I will teach you. Hear my words with deep attention."
6. "In truth, it is not for love of a husband that a husband is dear. It is for the love of the soul in the husband that a husband is dear.
7. It is not for the love of a wife that a wife is dear. It is for the love of the soul within the wife that a wife is dear."
8. It is not for the love of children that children are dear. It is for the love of the soul in the children that children are dear.

9. It is not for the love of riches that riches are dear. It is for the love of the soul in riches that riches are dear.
10. It is not for the love of religion that religion is dear. It is for the love of the soul in religion that religion is dear.
11. It is not for the love of power that power is dear. It is for the love of the soul in power that power is dear.
12. It is not for the love of the heavens that the heavens are dear. It is for the love of the soul in the heavens that the heavens are dear.
13. It is not for the love of the gods that the gods are dear. It is for the love of the soul in the gods that the gods are dear.
14. It is not for the love of creatures that creatures are dear. It is for the love of the soul in creatures that creatures are dear.
15. It is not for the love of the all that the all is dear. It is for the love of the soul in the all that the all is dear.
16. It is the soul, the spirit and the self that must be seen and heard and have our thoughts and meditations, O Sophia.
17. When the soul is seen and heard, is thought of and known, all that is becomes known.
18. Religion will abandon the one who thinks that religion is apart from the soul.
19. The gods will abandon the one who thinks the gods are apart from the soul.
20. Creatures will abandon the one who thinks creatures are apart from the soul.
21. And all will abandon the one who thinks that the all is apart from the soul.

22. Because religion, power, heavens, beings and gods rest in the soul.
23. When a drum is being beaten, its rhythm cannot be held. By seizing the drum or even the beater, the rhythm is held.
24. When the conch is being blown, its sounds cannot be held. By seizing the conch or even the blower, the sounds are held.
25. When a pipe is being smoked, its smoke cannot be held. By seizing the pipe or the smoker, the smoke is held. So it is with the Spirit.
26. When a lump of salt is cast into the water and therein dissolved, it cannot be grasped again. But wherever the water is taken, there is found salt."
27. Likewise, O Sophia, the Spirit is an ocean of pure consciousness; it is boundless and infinite. It arises out of the elements and returns to them. There is no consciousness after death."
28. "I am amazed, O Lord," exclaimed Sophia, "that after death, there is no consciousness."
29. To this, Michael replied, "I am not speaking to astound. Sufficient for wisdom is what I speak.
30. For where there seems to be a duality, one sees another, hears another and knows another. But when all has become Spirit, how and whom would one see?
31. How and whom would one hear? How and whom would one smell? How and to whom would one speak? How and whom would one know? How can one know him who knows all? How can the knower be known?"

Thou art Adam.

CHAPTER THIRTY-TWO

1. TO King David, came the wise saint Michael. He meant to bid him farewell to a life of meditation and renunciation. He felt the Spirit of Adam quickening him, and he felt his waiting was almost in fullness.
2. The king was distraught because another war was approaching. It was bigger than what he had ever experienced. His kingdom hung in the balance, and he sought his teacher and friend for guidance.
3. King David hugged his brother and asked this question: "Master, what is the light of man?"
4. "The sun is the light, O king," he answered. "It is by that light that one rests, goes forth, does his work and returns.
5. "This is the truth, David. And when the sun is set, what then becomes man's light?"
6. "The moon becomes his light," the king replied. "It is through the light of the moon that a man rests, goes forth, does his work and returns."
7. "This is true, David. And when the sun and the moon are set, what becomes man's light?"
8. "Fire then becomes his light. It is through the fire's light that a man rests, goes forth, does his work and returns."
9. "And when the sun and the moon are set and the fire has sunk down, what becomes man's light?"

10. "The voice becomes his light. Through the voice, he rests, goes forth, does his work and returns. Therefore, when a man cannot see even his own hand, if he hears a voice, he drifts after that way."
11. "That is the truth. And when the sun and moon are set, the fire sunk low and the voice is silent, what then, becomes man's light?"
12. "The soul becomes his light. Through that light, he rests, goes forth, does his work and returns."
13. "What then is the soul?" asked the king.
14. "It is the consciousness of life. It is the light of the heart. Forever remaining the same, the Spirit of Adam wanders in the real world and the dreamer's world.
15. He seems to wander in thought. He seems to wander in joy.
16. But in deep sleep, He goes beyond this world and its feeling forms.
17. When the Spirit in one comes to life and takes a body, one is joined with mortal evils. But when at death one goes beyond, one leaves evil behind.
18. The Spirit in men has two dwellings: this world and the world beyond. There is also a third dwelling place: the land of sleep, meditation, imagination and dreams.
19. Resting in this borderland, the Spirit in men can behold his dwelling in this world and in other worlds afar off. Wandering in this borderland, He beholds behind him the sorrows of this world. In front of him, He sees the joys of the beyond."
20. And Michael fell back into a meditative slumber; he convulsed though not violently. When he was aroused, his face grew loving and he spoke further:

21. "When the Spirit of man rests, He takes with Him materials from this all-containing world. He creates and destroys in his own glory and radiance. The Spirit of man then shines in His own light.
22. In that land, there are no ships; there are no oceans or waves. He creates His own ships, oceans and waves.
23. There are no joys in that region, and He creates His own joys.
24. On those shores, there are no lakes, ponds or streams. He creates His own lakes, ponds, and streams. For the Spirit of man is the Creator.
25. Abandoning His body by the gate of dreams, the Spirit beholds in awakening his senses sleeping. Then He takes His own light and returns to His home, this spirit of golden radiance, the wandering awareness everlasting.
26. Leaving His nest in charge of the breath of life, the Immortal Spirit soars afar from it.
27. He moves wherever He loves.
28. And in the regions of dreams, wandering above and below, the spirit makes innumerable creations.
29. Sometimes, He seems to rejoice in the love of fairy beauties. Sometimes, He laughs or beholds awe-inspiring visions. People see His ocean of pleasure, but He can never be seen.
30. Scoffers say that one should not suddenly awaken a person, for hard to heal would one be if the Spirit did not return.
31. They also say that dreams are like being awake, for what is seen when one is awake is seen again in a dream. The truth is that the Spirit shines in His own light.

32. When the Spirit of man has had joy in the land of dreams; when, in his wanderings, there has been good and evils, he returns to the world of waking. But whatever he has seen does not return with him, for the Spirit in man is free.
33. And when he has had his joy in this world of waking and in his wanderings here; when he has experienced good and evil, he returns by the same path to the land of dreams.
34. A great fish swims along the two banks of a river, first along the eastern bank and then along the western bank. In the same way, the Spirit of Adam moves beside his two dwellings: the waking world and the land of dreams.
35. After soaring in the sky, a falcon or bird of prey folds her wings for she is weary; she flies down to her nest. Likewise, the Spirit of man hastens to that place of rest where the soul has no desires and the Spirit sees no dreams.
36. What was seen in a dream is seen to be a delusion.
37. But when the Spirit feels "I am all," He is in the highest world where there are no desires. All evil has vanished, and there is no fear.
38. A man in the arms of a beloved woman feels only peace all around him. In the same way, the Soul in the embrace of Adam feels only peace all around. All desires are attained. No desires are there, and there is no sorrow.
39. There, a father is a father no more just like a mother is no longer a mother. The worlds are no longer the worlds; the gods are no longer gods.
40. There, the Scriptures disappear. A thief is not a thief, nor is the slayer a slayer. The outcast is not an outcast, nor is the beggar in poverty. The pilgrim is not a pilgrim, and the hermit is not a

hermit. Because the Spirit of Adam has crossed the lands of good and evil and passed beyond the sorrows of the heart.

41. There, the Spirit sees not. But through seeing not, He sees. How could the Spirit not see He is the all? But there is no duality there. There is nothing apart from Himself to see.

42. There, the Spirit smells no scents, yet He feels them. How could the Spirit feel no scents if He is the all? But there is no duality there. There are no scents apart from Himself to feel.

43. There, the Spirit tastes not, yet He tastes. How could the Spirit not taste if He is the all? But there is no duality there. There is nothing apart from Himself to taste.

44. The Spirit speaks not, yet He speaks. How could He not speak if He is the all? But there is no duality there. There is nothing apart from Himself to speak to.

45. There, the Spirit hears not, yet He hears. How could the Spirit not hear if He is the all? But there is no duality there. There is nothing apart from Himself to hear.

46. There, the Spirit thinks not, yet He thinks. How could the Spirit not think if He is the all? But there is no duality there. There is nothing apart from Himself to think.

47. There, the Spirit touches not, yet He touches. How could the Spirit not touch if he is the all? But there is no duality there. There is nothing apart from Himself to touch.

48. There, the Spirit knows not, yet He knows. How could the Spirit not know if He is the all? But there is no duality there. There is nothing apart from Himself to know.

49. Where there seems to be a duality, one sees another. One feels the perfume of another. One tastes another. One speaks to another. One listens to another. One touches another, and one knows another.
50. But in the ocean of the Spirit, the seer is alone as beholds His own immensity.
51. This world is the mind of Adam, O king. This is the supreme course. This is the supreme treasure. This is the supreme world. This is the supreme joy. On a portion of that joy, all other beings live.
52. One who is in this world attains success and pleasure, who is the Lord of men and enjoys all human pleasures, has reached the supreme human joy.
53. But a hundred times greater than the human joy is the joy of those who have attained the heaven of the ancestors.
54. A hundred times greater than the heaven of the ancestors is the joy of the heaven of the celestial beings.
55. A hundred times greater than the joy of the heaven of the celestial beings is the joy of the gods who have attained divinity through holy works.
56. A hundred times greater than the joy of the gods who have attained divinity through holy works is the joy of the gods who were born divine; the joy of one who has sacred wisdom; joy of one who is pure and free from desire.
57. A hundred times greater than the joy of the gods who were born divine is the joy of the world of the Lord of creation; the joy of one who has sacred wisdom, is pure and free from desire.
58. A hundred times greater than the joy of the Lord of creation is the joy of the world of Adam; the joy

of one who has sacred wisdom, is pure and free from desire.
59. This is supreme joy. This is the world of the Spirit, O king."
60. The wiseard spoke further. "When the Spirit in man has had his joy in the land of dreams, in his wanderings and there has beholden good and evil, he returns to this world of the awake.
61. A heavy-laden cart proceeds with aching, creaking, and groaning. Likewise, the body moves aches and groans when a man is giving up the breath of life.
62. When the body gets weak due to old age or disease, the Spirit of Adam is released from it. The Spirit returns by the same way of life, wherefrom He came.
63. When a king is approaching, his nobles, officers, admirals and the heads of the city prepare his meals and royal accommodations. "The king is approaching! The king is coming!" They all shout.
64. In the same way, all the powers of life wait for him who knows this. "The Spirit is approaching! The Spirit is coming!" They say.
65. When a king is going to depart, his nobles, officers, admirals and the heads of the city assemble about him.
66. Even so, all the powers of life gather about the soul when a man is giving up the breath of life.
67. When the human soul weakens and loses consciousness, all the powers of life assemble around. The soul gathers the elements of life and enters into the heart. And when the Spirit that lives behind the eye has returned to His own source, the soul knows no more forms.

68. One's powers of life become one and people say, "He sees no more."
69. His powers of life become one and they say, "He smells no more."
70. His powers of life become one and they say, "He tastes no more."
71. His powers of life become one and they say, "He speaks no more."
72. His powers of life become one and they say, "He hears no more."
73. His powers of life become one and they say, "He thinks no more."
74. His powers of life become one and they say, "He touches no more.
75. His powers of life become one and they say, "He knows no more."
76. At the point of the heart, the light of Adam shines forth and illuminates the soul on its course. When departing by the head, eye or mind, life arises and follows the soul. The powers of life follow, and the soul becomes conscious. His wisdom and works take him by the hand.
77. When a caterpillar comes atop a blade of grass, it stretches itself out and draws itself onto another blade. In the same way, when the soul leaves the body and ignorance behind, it reaches out to another body and draws itself to it.
78. A goldsmith takes an old ring and melts it before molding it into a new and fairer form. Likewise, the soul leaves the body and ignorance behind before going into a new and fairer form that is full of glory. The form is like that of the ancestors in heaven, celestial beings, gods of light or the Lord of creation.
79. The soul is Adam.

80. He is made of consciousness and mind. He is made of life and vision.
81. He is made from the earth and the waters. He is made from air and space.
82. He is made from light and darkness. He is made from desire and peace.
83. He is made from anger and love. He is made from virtue and vice.
84. He is made up of all that is near. He is made up of all that is afar. He is made of all.
85. One who is free from desire, whose desire finds fulfillment, since the Spirit is one's desire, the powers of life leave not such a one, becomes one with Adam, the Spirit.
86. When all the heart's desires disappear, a mortal becomes immortal. Even in this life, he attains freedom.
87. As the shed skin of a snake lies on the ground, so too does the human body. But the incorporeal Spirit is life and light and eternity."
88. I have found the narrow path, known of old that stretches far away. Through it, saints who know the Spirit rise to the heavens.
89. It is singing with rainbow light. This is the path to eternity for the seers of Adam whose actions are pure and who have inner fire and light."
90. Into deep darkness, fall those who follow the course of action. Into deeper darkness, fall those who follow the course of knowledge.
91. There are worlds of no joy—regions of utter darkness. Those who have created torment for themselves go to those worlds upon death.
92. When awake to the vision of Adam; when one can say, "I am He," what desires could lead one to grieve for the body?

93. To him who has found Adam and awakened to His light, belongs the world of the Spirit who is the world.
94. While we are here in this life, we may reach the light of wisdom. And if we reach it not, how deep is the darkness!
95. Those who see the light enter into eternity. Those who live in darkness enter into self-destructive sorrow.
96. When one sees Adam, one fears no more.
97. Before whom the years roll and all the days of the years, Him the gods adore as the Light of all lights, as Life Immortal.
98. He is Adam the immortal, in whom the five hosts of being rest. He is the Eternal Spirit.
99. Those who know Him who is the eye of the eye; the ear of the eye; the mind of the mind and the life of life, know Adam from the beginning of time.
100. Even by the mind, this truth must be seen: there are not many but only one; whoever sees variety and not the unity wanders in self-created delusion.
101. Behold the eternal One who radiates beyond space.
102. Knowing this, let the lover of Adam follow wisdom. Let not the mind ponder on many words, for many words bring weariness.
103. This is the great Adam. He dwells in our own great hearts as Ruler of all.
104. His greatness becomes greater not by good actions; it does not become less great by evil actions. He is the Lord, protector of all beings. He is the rainbow bridge that keeps the worlds apart lest they fall into confusion.

105. The lovers of Adam seek Him through the sacred Scriptures, charity, penance, fasting, prayer and worship.
106. He who knows Adam becomes a wiseard. Pilgrims follow their life of wandering as they long for His kingdom.
107. Knowing this, the saints of old desired not even offspring. Rising above the desire for sons, wealth and the world, they followed the life of the pilgrim.
108. For the desire of sons and wealth is a desire for the world. This desire is vanity among vanities.
109. The Spirit of Adam is not vanity. He is incomprehensible. He is imperishable. He has no bonds of attachment; He is free from all bonds and is beyond suffering and fear.
110. One who knows this is not moved by grief or exultation on account of evil or good one has done. He goes beyond both. He does not grieve what is done or left undone.
111. The everlasting greatness of a beholder of Adam is not greater or less great through actions. Let a man find the path of the Spirit. He who finds this path becomes free from the bonds of evil."
112. He who knows this and has found peace is Lord of himself. In Himself, one sees the Spirit as all.
113. He is not moved by evil; He removes evil. He is not burned by sin; He burns all sin. And He goes beyond all evil—all passion and all doubt—because He sees the eternal. This is the world of the Spirit, O king.
Thou art Adam."

CHAPTER THIRTY-THREE

1. MICHAEL lifted up his eyes to heaven. "Adam, the hour has come. Glorify thy soul so that it may glorify thee.
2. As thou has given me power over all flesh so that I should give eternal life to as many as thou has given me.
3. And this is eternal life that they might know thee—the only true God and my highest self—whom thou has sent.
4. I have glorified thee on the earth. I have finished the work which thou gave me to do. And now, O Lord Adam, glorify thou me with your own self with the glory which I had with thee before the world was.
5. I have manifested thy name unto the men which thou gave me out of the world. Yours they were; thou gave them to me, and they have kept thy word.
6. Now they have known that all things thou has given me are of thee.
7. For I have given unto them the words which thou gave me. They have received them and have surely known that I came out from thee. They have believed that thou did send me.
8. I pray for them everywhere and every time. I pray not for the world itself, but for them which thou

has given me. All who are mine are yours. All who are yours are mine. I am glorified in them.

9. And now I am no more in the world. But these are in the world, and I come to thee. Holy Father Adam, keep through your own name those whom thou has given me so that they may be one, as we are.

10. While I was with them in the world, I kept them in thy name. Those that thou gave me, I have kept; none but the son of perdition is lost so that the scripture might be fulfilled.

11. And now I come to thee. These things I speak in the world so that they might have my joy fulfilled in themselves.

12. I have given them thy word. The world hath hated them because they are not of the world just like I am not of the world.

13. I pray not that thou should take them out of the world but that thou should keep them from the evil within themselves.

14. They are not of the world like I am not of the world.

15. Enlighten them through thy truth. Thy word is truth.

16. As thou has sent me into the world, I also sent them into the world.

17. And for their sakes, I have enlightened myself so that they also might be enlightened through the truth.

18. Neither pray I for these alone but for them also which shall believe me through their word so that they all may be one. As thou art in me and I in thee, may they be one in us so that the world may believe that thou has sent me.

19. And the glory which thou gave me I have given them so that they may be one like we are one.
20. I am in them, and they art in me so that they may be made perfect in one and that the world may know that thou has sent me and has loved them as thou has loved me.
21. Lord Adam, I will that they also, whom thou has given me. Be with me where I am so that they may behold my glory which thou has given me. For thou loved me before the foundation of the world.
22. O righteous Adam, the world hath not known thee, not yet. But I have known thee, and these have known that thou has sent me.
23. And I have declared unto them thy name and will declare it so that the love wherewith thou has loved me may be in them, and I in them. Thou art Adam."
24. As Michael and the king were walking along and talking together, a chariot of fire drawn by horses of flame appeared. It separated the two of them and Michael went up to heaven in a whirlwind.
25. "O Lord Adam," said King David, "Yours is my kingdom, and I am Yours forever."
26. Uncovered and without reserve, King David danced before the Lord Adam. He led his kingdom in righteous light.
27. Overcoming wars and accosting many threats, Lord Adam preserved King David's domain, for David was a man after His heart.
28. This is the Spirit of Lord Adam, the enjoyer of the food of life and giver of treasure. He who knows this finds this treasure.
29. This is the Spirit of Adam which is never old and is utterly immortal. This is the Spirit of the universe, a refuge from all fear. Thou art Adam.

THE TESTAMENT OF ADAM
BOOK TWO

CHAPTER ONE

1. KING David saw the sons of Adam standing ready as his enemies. The greatest war of his reign was about to begin with the hurling of mighty weapons. The king, whose banner bore the emblem of Lord Adam, took up his bow and prayed fervently to Lord Adam.
2. Having been invoked by David, Lord Adam summoned His archangel. Michael swept David up a radiant chariot of fire. He knelt down and began to speak. "Lord, open his eyes so that he may see all."
3. And the king's eyes were opened to a place between places. His senses were opened to all manner of fiery chariots, demonic beasts, angels and spirits. Wheels turning with spikes and weapons of war. Armies gathered in realms unseen by the natural eye. Legions of powers stretched out in every dimension, ready to battle.
4. His mind grasped for understanding. Michael was now transfigured; he stood erect with a shining, golden body. His eyes were like lightning, and his head tilted back at the thundering sky. He was possessed by the Spirit of Adam.
5. Then the Spirit of Adam drove the chariot into the place before the two armies. The souls of the Lord

confronted the dark rulers of the earth and below the earth; of the armies of the darkness of man's heart, that old serpent of deceit and lies.
6. The great bulls of Bashan stamped and snorted smoke from their nostrils. And he saw the faces of malice and pride stretch on endlessly from every direction. The faces of all those who wished death upon him.
7. Enemies of both carnal natures, principalities and powers now engulfed him and his chariot of Holy Fire. "O David," said Michael, "behold the assembled legions!" The heat from the hatred that emanated from him caused him to sweat heavy and salty drops of blood.
8. As he looked on, he saw familiar faces in both armies: fathers, grandfathers, fathers-in-law, dear friends and many others. And as his kinsmen and followers flashed before his vision, his face went pale. He was filled with deep compassion and spoke despairingly.
9. "My Lord, seeing my friends and relatives before me in such a fighting spirit, I feel the limbs of my body quivering as my mouth dries up. My whole body is trembling. My hair is standing on end. My bow is slipping from my hand. My skin is burning. I am now unable to stand here any longer. I am forgetting myself, and my mind is reeling.
10. I see only the causes of misfortune. I do not see how any good can come from killing my own kinsmen in this battle. In this way, I cannot desire victory, kingdom or happiness.
11. What good is a kingdom, happiness or even life itself when all the elders, friends and relatives are dead? For whom we desire the kingdom,

enjoyments, and pleasures? I foresee no good by slaying my own people in the fight.

12. When teachers and relatives are ready to give up their lives or properties and are standing before me, why would I wish to kill them?
13. I am not prepared to fight them even in exchange for the universe, let alone this earth.
14. What pleasure will we derive from killing these people? Sin will overcome us if we slay such people.
15. It is not proper for us to kill these people. How could we be happy by killing our own kinsmen?
16. Lord Adam, hearing the prayers of all men, tell me how we can hope to be happy after damning even the sons of deceit. Evil they may be, but if we damn them, is our sin not greater?
17. How could we dare spill the blood that unites us? Must we not shun this crime, O Father of Life?
18. We know what fate falls on lineages of the broken. The vows are forgotten. Vice rots the remnant and defile the women. Their corruption brings the storms of lust and the curse of confusion which degrades the victims and damns the destroyers.
19. No longer shall bread and wine be offered. The damned ancestors must also fall from eternity in heaven. Such is the crime of the killers of kinsmen. The sacred ancient is broken and forgotten.
20. Darkness, doubting and hell: such is the doom of those lost without salvation. What is this judgment we are planning, O Father?
21. Damnation and perdition most hateful; the annihilation of brothers. Indeed, am I so glorious for greatness?

22. Rather than this, let sons of perdition come at me with weapons. I shall not struggle. I shall not strike them. Let them kill me, for that will be better."
23. After saying this, David put aside his bow and arrows. With his mind full of sorrow, he sat down in the back of the chariot. He was reluctant to fight.

CHAPTER TWO

1. DAVID'S eyes were tearful and downcast. He was overwhelmed by compassion and despair. Michael fell back and uttered the voice of Lord Adam. The Spirit of the Lord thundered to David:
2. "O king of men, is this the time for scruples and fancies? Are they worthy of you, those who seek to follow the will of the Father?
3. Any brave hero who hopes to see God would despise them. What is this weakness? It is beneath you! How has the dejection come to you at this juncture?
4. This is not fit for a person of noble mind and knowledge. It is disgraceful, and it does not lead one to fame, O David. Is it for nothing that men call you the king? Shake off this cowardice; do not yield to its impotence. Gird thy loins and stand up for battle!"
5. David said, "How shall I strike my kinsmen, O Lord Adam?
6. It would be better, indeed, to be a beggar than to win the kingdom by slaying these noble personalities. By killing them, all I would get is wealth and pleasures stained with their blood.
7. And David wept blood. "The Principalities of this world are so ancient and profane; they are worthy

of the deepest terror. How can I greet such fiery darts in battle?

8. If I slay all of them, how can I enjoy my wealth and glory?

9. It will be stained with blood guilt. I would rather spare them and eat the bread of a beggar!

10. I do not think that gaining an unrivaled and prosperous kingdom will remove the sin I would be committing in killing them. We may not even wish to live after killing our cousins and brothers, who are standing in front of us.

11. Is this real compassion I feel, Father? Is it only a delusion? My mind gropes about in darkness. I cannot see where my duty lies. Father, I beg You to tell me clearly and frankly what I must do. I am your humble servant. I put myself in your hand, Father. Show me the way. I am Your disciple. I take refuge in You."

12. The Lord answered him, "Your words are wise, but your sorrow is in vain. Those wise ones who belong to the Kingdom of Adam do not mourn the living or the dead. There was never a time when I did not exist. There is no future in which I shall cease to be.

13. Just as The dweller in this body passes through childhood, youth, and into old age; so, at death, he merely passes into another kind of body. The faithful are not deceived by that. The contacts of the senses with the sense objects give rise to the feelings of pain and pleasure. They are transitory. All arise from sense perception.

14. While performing one's duty, one may learn to tolerate them without being disturbed.

15. Only persons who are not disturbed by either happiness or distress are fit to become immortal.

16. A faithful spirit serenely accepts pleasure and pain with an even mind; it is unmoved by either. He is worthy of the immortality of God.
17. The physical body dies. Only the Holy Spirit of Adam is eternal. Adam is indestructible.
18. In this way, you and the others are all Adam. The Spirit neither slays nor is slain. If you think you are slaying others, you are ignorant.
19. The Spirit is neither born nor does it die when the body dies.
20. David, how can a person who knows that the Spirit is indestructible kill anyone or have anyone killed? Some say this Spirit is slain; others call it the slayer. They know nothing. How can it slay? Who shall slay it? Therefore, you must fight, O David!
21. Know thy Spirit. How can it die the death of the body?
22. Dream not that you do the deed of the killer the works of the judge. Dream not that the burden is yours to command it.
23. Worn-out garments are shed by the body as old wineskins. Worn out bodies are shed by the dweller within the body.
24. New bodies are donned by the Spirit like garments. They are not wounded by weapons, burned by fire, dried by the wind or drenched by water.
25. Such is the Holy Spirit: not dried, not wet, unburned, not wounded, being of beings, changeless and eternal.
26. Knowing the permanence of the Spirit, grieve not.
27. Be aware that death is certain for the one who is born, and birth is certain for the one who dies.

Therefore, you may not lament over the inevitable.
28. The Holy Spirit cannot be grasped by the mind. It is not subject to modification. Since you know this, you may not grieve.
29. But if one does suppose that the Spirit is subject to constant birth and death, one ought not to be sorry. Death is certain for the born; resurrection is certain for the dead.
30. Before birth, man's senses are not manifested. Between birth and death, they are manifested. Upon death, they return to the unmanifested again. What in all this is there to mourn over? You may not grieve over that which is unavoidable.
31. There have been some, chosen by God, who have assuredly looked upon the Spirit and understood Him in all His wonder. Others can only speak of Him as wonderful beyond all understanding. Others only know of the wonder by preaching, yet others are told of it and do not understand a word.
32. David, the Holy Spirit that dwells in the body of all beings remains eternally indestructible. Therefore, you may not mourn for anybody."
33. Considering your duty as a warrior, you may not waver like this. There is nothing more auspicious for a warrior than a righteous war. There is no need for hesitation.
34. Only the fortunate warriors get the opportunity for an unsought war that is like an open door to heaven.
35. Even if thou consider the dilemma from a standpoint of duty, you may not hesitate. What is more assured and noble than a righteous war for a warrior?

36. Happy are warriors to whom a battle such as this comes. Such a battle opens the door to heaven.
37. If you refuse to fight in this righteous war, you will be turning from the will of God. You will be a disgraced sinner.
38. People will speak ill of you throughout the ages. To a man that values the eternal, surely this is worse than death.
39. The elect will think it was fear which drove you from battle. You will be despised by those who have admired you for so long.
40. Your enemies also will slander your courage. To the honored, dishonor is worse than death. What could be worse to bear than that?
41. You will either go to heaven if killed in the line of duty, or you will enjoy the kingdom on the earth if victorious. Therefore, get up with a determination to fight, O David.
42. Die and you win the keys to the kingdom of God. Conquer and you will enjoy the earth. Stand up now as a soldier of Adam; shore up your resolve.
43. Before going into battle, realize that pleasure and pain, gain and loss or victory and defeat are all one and the same. Do this and you will not commit any sin.
44. I have explained to you the true nature of the Spirit. Now listen to the wisdom of the righteous path which, if you can follow it, will help you break the chains of temptation which bind you to your actions.
45. On this path, even a short distance traveled is never wasted. Every step gets you closer to Eve's wheel of carnal birth and death.

46. On this path, the will is directed toward one ideal. When a man lacks this discrimination, his will wanders in all directions after innumerable aims.
47. Those who lack discrimination may quote the letter of the Scripture, but they are really denying its truth. They are full of worldly desires and hunger for the rewards of heaven.
48. They use beautiful figures of speech. They teach elaborate rituals which are supposed to give pleasure and power to those who perform them. However, they understand nothing but the law of condemnation which chains men to eternal suffering.
49. There are many people who consider the Scriptures as containing only rituals from which to derive heavenly enjoyment.
50. They are the people who are misguided. They merely chant the Scriptures without understanding their real purpose. They do not get any self-realization through ritualistic activities.
51. Those whose discrimination is stolen by such talk grow deeply attached to pleasure and power. They are unable to develop the concentration of will and the discipline of character which leads to admission into Adam's kingdom.
52. All the Scriptures essentially teach about the three aspects of Eve: light, fire and darkness. Light represents pure goodness and righteousness. Fire represents burning passion. Darkness represents chaotic and destructive ignorance.
53. But there is a realm beyond the Scriptures which makes you lead a balanced life. It helps you rise above the anxieties of acquisition and preservation.

54. You, O son of Adam, must overcome these three aspects of Eve. Let your mind be tranquil. Be established in the consciousness of the Adam, and walk with the Holy Spirit.
55. To a self-realized person who has risen above the Scriptures, the words are as useful as a small stream of water when water from a huge lake becomes available.
56. When the entire land is flooded, even the lake becomes superfluous. Likewise, to those who have obtained the salvation of God, all the Scriptures are superfluous.
57. You have a right to perform your prescribed duty, but you are not entitled to the fruits of your action. Never consider yourself the cause of the results of your activities. Never be attached to not doing your duty.
58. You have control over doing your duty only; you have no control over the results.
59. You have the right to work, but the desire for the fruits of the work must never be the motive.
60. Do your duty to the best of your ability, with your mind attached to the Lord. Abandon worry or selfish attachment to the results.
61. The selfless service is worship that brings peace and equanimity of mind. Perform every action with your heart fixed on Adam. Give the fruits to God.
62. Be even-tempered in success and failure. Such peace is manifested by the Holy Spirit.
63. In the calm of self-surrender, you can free yourself from the bondage of virtue and vice in this life.
64. Devote yourself to walking in union with the Lord. To unite the heart with the Spirit and to act

accordingly, that is the secret of non-attached work.
65. In the calm of self-surrender, the devout renounce the fruit of their actions and reach salvation.
66. They are free from the bondage of hell; they pass into that state which is beyond all evil.
67. When your mind has cleared itself of all delusions, you become indifferent to the results of all actions.
68. The confused mind is bewildered by conflicting interpretations of the Scriptures. When it can steadily rest while contemplating on the Spirit, then he will reach union with the Holy Spirit.
69. One engaged in devotional service rids himself of good and bad actions. Work done with selfish motives is inferior to selfless services.
70. Therefore, be a selfless worker. Those who work only to enjoy the fruits of their labor are unhappy because one has no control over the results.
71. And David asked, "Lord, how can one identify a man who is firmly established and absorbed into the Spirit?
72. How does such a person live in this world?"
73. And the Angel of the Lord replied, "He knows the bliss in the Spirit and wants nothing else. He renounces the cravings tormenting his heart. I call him glorified.
74. He is not shaken by adversity. He does not yearn for happiness. He is free from fear, hunger and all his heart's desires. I call him blessed and illumined.
75. The bonds of his flesh are broken. He is lucky and does not rejoice. He is unlucky and does not weep. I call him glorified.
76. When one can completely withdraw the senses from the sense objects as a tortoise withdraws its

limbs into the shell, the intellect of such a person is considered steady.

77. The true believer can draw in his senses I call him glorified.
78. The abstinent flee from that which they desire but carry their desires with them. When a man truly enters union with the Spirit, he leaves his burdens behind him.
79. Thus, a person whose mind is unperturbed by sorrow; does not crave pleasures; is completely free from attachment, fear and anger is a person of steady intellect.
80. He may be a person who is neither elated by getting desired results nor perturbed by any undesired results.
81. When one is completely free from all desires of the mind and is satisfied with the Supreme Being, he is called an enlightened person.
82. Even a mind which knows the narrow path can be dragged from that path. The senses of man are so unruly. But the faithful controls the senses, recollects the mind and fixes it on me. I call him faithful.
83. The senses are so strong, impetuous and restless that they may forcibly carry away the mind of even the wisest person striving for perfection.
84. One develops an attachment to sense objects by thinking about sense objects. The desire for sense objects comes from the attachment to sense objects. Anger comes from the unfulfilled desires. When one grows attached, he becomes addicted.
85. Thwart your addiction and it turns to anger which confounds the mind; delusion and wild ideas arise from anger. The mind is bewildered by delusion.

Reasoning is destroyed when the mind is bewildered.

86. To confuse one's mind is to forget the lesson from the experience. To forget the experience is to lose discrimination. Lose discrimination, and one misses life's only purpose. One falls down from the right path when reasoning is destroyed.

87. One's intellect becomes steady when his senses are under control. One may fix his mind on God after bringing the senses under control.

88. When he has no lust or hatred, one walks safely among the things of lust and hatred. Obeying the Spirit is one's peaceful joy. Sorrow melts into that clear peace. Ones' quiet mind is soon established in peace.

89. The wind turns a ship from its course. In the same way, the wandering winds of the senses cast a man's mind adrift and turn his better judgment from its course.

90. The mind, when controlled by the roving senses, steals the intellect like a storm takes away a boat on the sea from its destination.

91. When one can still his senses, I call him liberated. The recollected mind is awake in the knowledge of the Spirit.

92. The ignorant are awake in their sense-life which they think is their daylight. To the seer of the Lord, it is darkness.

93. The saint remains alert when everyone is asleep. And when everyone is awake, he still sees them as asleep.

94. Water flows continually into the ocean, yet the ocean is never disturbed Desire flows into the mind of the saint, but he is never disturbed.

95. One who desires material objects is never at peace. Only the one who abandons all desires and longings attains peace.
96. The man who stirs up his own lust can never know peace. He who knows peace lives without craving. He is free from his ego or pride.
97. All sorrows are destroyed upon attainment of tranquility. This is the state of walking in unison with the Lord Almighty.
98. David, this is the ascended state of mind. When one attains this state, he is no longer deluded and is one with the Absolute.
99. One does not fall back into delusion. Even at death, he is alive in that salvation. He is one with the Lord."

CHAPTER THREE

1. DAVID asked, "But Father, if you consider the knowledge of the Holy Spirit superior to any sort of action, why are you telling me to do these terrible deeds? Your statements seem to contradict each other. They confuse my mind. If that knowledge alone is important, why should I engage in a war? Tell me one definite way to reach the righteousness of God."
2. And the angel of the Lord spoke, "I have already told you that in this world, aspirants may attain enlightenment through two different paths. For the contemplative, is the path of knowledge. For the action, is the path of selfless action or service.
3. Whatever path one may take, one has to do his duty to attain freedom from the bondage of duty. No one can get this freedom from past duty by simply abstaining from work. One does not attain fulfillment by simple renunciation.
4. Freedom from activity is never achieved by abstaining from action. Nobody can become perfect by merely ceasing to act. In fact, no one can ever rest from his activity. All are helplessly forced to act by the flesh.
5. No one can remain without doing work even for a moment. Even the maintenance of your body would not be possible without work.

6. Activity is better than inertia. Act but with self-control. If you are lazy, you cannot sustain your own body.
7. While working is better than sitting idle, between people who work, the one who learns to control his emotions and engages in selfless service is considered superior. His work is for the Creator; he is free from any selfish attachment to the fruits of his work.
8. A man who renounces certain physical actions but still lets his mind dwell on the objects of his sensual desire is only deceiving himself. He can only be called a hypocrite.
9. The truly admirable man controls his senses by the power of the Spirit within him. All his actions are disinterested. All are directed along the path to union with the Lord.
10. The world is imprisoned by its own activity, except when the actions are performed in worship of God. Therefore, you must perform every action sacramentally; you must be free from all attachments to results.
11. In the beginning, Adam created human beings together with selfless service to each other. The Lord of beings created all men to each his duty. "Do this," He said, "and you shall prosper." Duty done well fulfills all desire. Performing one's duty honors the Lord. To you, the Lord will be gracious. By serving each other they are all supposed to prosper. When people serve each other, they nourish each other and are nourished by Adam. The supreme goal is to be attained by nourishing one another. By honoring each other, man reaches the Highest. Please the Lord, and your prayer will be granted. But he who enjoys the bounty of the

Spirit and shows no thanksgiving, thieves from the Almighty.
12. The devout are sinless and eat what the Lord leaves after the offering. But those greedy heathens cooking choice food for their stomachs only sin as they eat it.
13. Everyone is supposed to eat only after feeding others—the celestial beings, gods, ancestors and angels—through ritual.
14. The angels, served by selfless people, will help them in their prosperity.
15. Those who eat after feeding others are freed from all sins. But the selfish eat their sin.
16. Food quickens the life-seed. It grows when the rain falls after sacrifices are offered to the heaven.
17. Sacrifice speaks through the act of ritual. Ritual is taught by the sacred Scriptures that spring from the lips of the Changeless One.
18. Rituals are prescribed in the Scriptures which are directly manifested from the supreme personality of the Godhead. Consequently, the all-pervading transcendence is eternally situated in acts of sacrifice.
19. Know therefore that Lord Adam is dwelling forever within this ritual.
20. If one plays no part in his acts thus appointed, one's very living is evil. Know this, O David, his life is for nothing.
21. But when one has found delight and satisfaction in the Spirit, one is no longer obliged to perform any actions. He has nothing to gain in this world by his actions.
22. One has nothing to lose by refraining from any action.

23. Do your duty always but without attachment to the results. That is how one stays in step with the Spirit.
24. Many saints reaped union with the Lord because they simply followed the will of the Spirit. Your motive in working may be to set others on the path of duty."
25. And the Lord spoke, "Whatever a great man does, ordinary people will imitate.
26. Consider Me. I am not bound by any sort of duty. There is nothing, in this realm or any other, that I do not already possess. I continue working, nevertheless.
27. If I did not continue to work tirelessly, mankind would still follow me wherever I led them.
28. Suppose I were to stop? They would all be lost. The result would be universal confusion and destruction.
29. The one who does not help to keep the wheel of creation in motion by performing his obligations is a selfish person. He is lost in the sea of vanity.
30. Thus, there is an obligation for everyone to participate in the design of Adam and to lead a life of contentment with the Supreme Being.
31. The ignorant work for the fruit of their action. The wise work without selfish desire.
32. Let the wise beware lest they bewilder the minds of the ignorant. Let them show, by example, how work is holy when the heart of the worker is fixated on the Highest.
33. As the ignorant work with attachment to the fruits of their work, the wise work without attachment. They work for the welfare of the society while leading people on the right path.

34. The forces of Mother Eve also perform their duties. Blessed is the one who knows the truth about the role of the forces of Mother Nature in completing their work.
35. Many times, it is the forces of nature that get their work done by using our organs as their instruments.
36. Every action is performed by the flesh. One deluded by the ego thinks he is the doer. One who has the eyes of the Lord has insight into reality and its various functions. He knows that when the senses attach themselves to objects, it is merely deluded perceptions attaching themselves to perceived delusions.
37. When you do your duty, it is the forces of Mother Nature that get the job done by you. Knowing this, a true disciple does not become attached to his actions.
38. When you refuse to do your duty, it is you who is acting and taking the blame.
39. Do your duty dedicating all works to God in a spiritual frame of mind that is free from desire, attachment and mental grief.
40. The disciple must not create confusion in the minds of the ignorant by refraining from work. The ignorant, in their delusion, identify the Spirit with the flesh. They become tied to the senses and actions of the senses.
41. Shake off this fever of ignorance. Stop hoping for worldly rewards. Fix your mind upon the Holy Spirit. Be free from the sense of self, and dedicate all your actions to me.
42. Those who faithfully practice this teaching and are free from evil become free from the bondage of

duty. But those who scoff at this teaching and do not practice it are ignorant, senseless and lost.
43. Do not be attached to your emotions. Your attachments and aversions are two major stumbling blocks on the path of your self-realization.
44. If a man follows my teaching, he will be released from his bonds of sin. Those who scorn my teaching are lost. They are without spiritual discrimination. All their knowledge is a delusion.
45. Even a wise man acts according to the propensities of his own nature. What use is any external restraint? The attractions and aversions which the senses feel for different objects are natural. But you must not give way to such propensities because they are obstacles.
46. It is better to do your own duty, however imperfectly, than to assume the duties of another person, however successfully. Prefer to die doing your own duty; the duty of another will cause great spiritual danger to befall you.
47. Therefore, O David, surrender all your works unto me. With full knowledge of me and without any desire for profit, fight!"
48. David asked, "O Adam, what impels one to do evil?
49. The angel of the Lord spoke unto him. "It is a passion of the flesh. From passion, the desire is born. The flesh has two faces: lust and rage. Recognize these for they are your enemies.
50. Smoke hides fire. Dust hides a mirror. The womb hides the embryo.
51. Lust hides the Spirit in its hungry flames. Intellect, senses, and the mind are fuel to its fire. Thus, it deludes the dweller in the body and bewilders his judgment.

52. Therefore, Son of Adam, you must control your senses. Kill this evil thing which obstructs discriminative knowledge and the realization of the Spirit.
53. Thus, self-knowledge gets covered by different degrees of this insatiable desire and eternal enemy of the wise.
54. Where does this desire reside? It resides in your senses, the mind and even in the intellect. It just deludes a person by covering his self-knowledge.
55. Therefore, O David, it is necessary to destroy this desire that destroys your self-knowledge and self-realization.
56. It is said that the senses are higher than the objects they perceive. The intelligent will is higher than the mind's comprehension. What is higher than the intelligent will? The Spirit Himself.
57. You must know Him who is above the intelligent will. Assume control of the mind through spiritual discrimination. Destroy the elusive enemy who wears the form of lust.

CHAPTER FOUR

1. MICHAEL, the angel of Lord Adam said, "Son of man, I have shown you the course that leads to the truth. I taught this truth to the first incarnation of Adam. Thus handed down in succession, the saintly kings knew this science of proper action.
2. In spiritual succession, Adam's truth carried onward from teacher to teacher until it was lost throughout ages forgotten. After a long time, science was lost to this earth.
3. Since you are my devotee and friend, I am describing the same to you."
4. Lord Adam said, "Both you and I have taken many births. I remember them all, O David, but you do not remember.
5. I am the Lord of all that breathes. I seem to be born. It is only seeming, only my nature. I am still master of my reality, the power that makes me.
6. Only the one who truly understands me, takes refuge in me and is freed from attachment, fear and anger. He becomes fully absorbed in my thoughts. He reaches my supreme abode after leaving his body. He does not take rebirth but is born as Lord Adam.
7. I am the eternal Lord of all beings. Whenever there is a decline of order, and chaos takes

predominance, I manifest myself. I appear from time to time to protect the good and to establish the world order.
8. When there is less good and evil prevails, I make myself a body. In every age, I come back to deliver the holy and destroy sin in order to establish righteousness.
9. Fleeing from fear, lust and anger, he takes refuge in me.
10. Whatever men pray for, I answer them. Whatever path men travel leads to me.
11. People worship me with different motives. Still, I accept them.
12. I am the composer of all kingdoms, rulers, principalities and powers which correspond to the various aspects of delusion and reality.
13. I am their author. However, I am changeless and beyond action.
14. Actions do not contaminate me. I have no desire at all for the fruits of action. A man who understands my nature in this respect will never become a slave to his own actions.
15. Because they understood this, saints, prophets and judges could safely engage in action. You also must do your work in the spirit of those ancient prophets.
16. What is action? What is inaction? Even the wise are confounded by this.
17. When you know that, you will be free from all impurity. You must learn what kind of work to perform, what kind of work to flee from, and how to reach a state of calm detachment from your work. The real nature of action is hard to understand.

18. He who sees the inaction within action and the action within inaction, is wise indeed. Even when he is engaged in action, he remains poised in the Spirit.
19. Assuredly, the prophets say that wise is he who acts without lust or scheming. His works fall from him. Its shackles are broken and melted in the flames of my knowledge.
20. Turning his face from the fruit, the Spirit is enough. He acts and is beyond action.
21. He calls nothing his own. He acts and does not sin.
22. What God's will gives, he takes and is contented. Pain follows pleasure, but he is not troubled. Gain follows loss, but he is indifferent. Of whom may he be jealous?
23. He acts, yet he is not bound by his action. When the bonds are broken, his illumined heart beats in the Spirit. His every action is worship of the Lord. Can such acts bring evil?
24. The Spirit is the ritual. The Spirit is the offering. The Spirit is the one who offers to the fire that is the Spirit.
25. If a man sees the Spirit in every action, he will find God.
26. Some who seek merely worship spirits and angels. Others, by the grace of God, are able to meditate on the identity of the Father, with the Spirit.
27. For these, the Spirit is the offering. The Lord is the sacrificial fire into which it is offered.
28. Some withdraw all their senses from contact with the exterior world and its objects. For these, hearing and the other senses are the offerings. Self-discipline is the sacrificial fire.
29. Others allow their minds and senses to wander unchecked. They try to see the Spirit within all

exterior sense objects. For these, sound and other sense objects are the offering. Sense enjoyment is the sacrificial fire.

30. Some renounce all the actions of the senses and all the functions of the vital force.
31. For these, such actions and functions are the offerings. The practice of self-control is the sacrificial fire which is kindled by knowledge of the Holy Spirit.
32. Then there are some, whose way of worship is to renounce sense objects and material possessions. Others set themselves austerities and spiritual disciplines: that is their way of worship.
33. Others worship through the practice of sacraments and rites. Others, who are earnest seekers for perfection and are men of strict vows, study and meditate on the truths of the Scriptures. That is their way of worship.
34. Others are intent on controlling the vital energy. They practice breathing exercises. Others mortify the flesh by fasting to weaken their sensual desires and achieve self-control.
35. All these understand the meaning of sacrifice and its form of worship. Through worship, their sins are consumed by the fire of the Lord.
36. What is common between all these men is they want to purify themselves by remaining selfless. They want to attain the Supreme Being. They understand that leading an attached life does not give happiness.
37. They consume the meat which has been blessed in the sacrifice. Thus, they obtain immortality and reach the eternal God.
38. He who does not worship God cannot be happy in this world. What can he expect from any other?

39. All these and many other forms of worship are prescribed by the Scriptures.
40. All of them involve doing some kind of action. When you fully understand this, you will be freed by the Spirit.
41. The form of worship which consists of contemplating on the Spirit is superior to ritualistic worship with material offerings.
42. A person walking with the Spirit sees action in inaction. He also sees inaction in action.
43. A person who meditates is engaged in action, though he appears not to be doing anything.
44. This saint finds no meaning in many actions that ordinary men are engaged in.
45. A person who does any action devoid of self-gratification and is selfless is a saint.
46. His work is free from desire. His attachment to the fruits of his actions are consumed in the fire of knowledge. He is an enlightened one.
47. Such a person is a contented person. The person who does not take shelter in the worldly things and abandons desires caused by action while engaged in work is not a doer.
48. He does all his duties in the name of God without attachment to the results.
49. A hangman does his job as per the orders of the king. Though he kills someone, he is not guilty because his actions are selfless and equivalent to inaction.
50. His mind and intellect are well-controlled. He acts without any desire or attachment.
51. A person who acts free from desire or attachment and in accordance with Lord Adam, does his work in service of the Lord.

52. He considers everything as an act of God. He is a saint.
53. The reward of all action is found in enlightenment.
54. Those illumined souls who have realized the truth will instruct you in the knowledge of the Spirit if you serve them as a disciple.
55. When you have reached enlightenment, ignorance will delude you no longer. In the light of that knowledge, you will see the entire creation within your own self and in me.
56. If you were the foulest of sinners, this knowledge alone would carry you like a raft over all of your sins.
57. The blazing fire turns wood to ashes the fire of knowledge turns all sins to ashes.
58. There is no purifier as great as this knowledge. When a man is made perfect in devotion, he knows its truth within his heart.
59. The man of faith, whose heart is devoted and whose senses are mastered, finds the Spirit. Enlightened, he passes to the Highest.
60. The ignorant goes to his destruction. How shall he enjoy this world, the next or any happiness?
61. When a man can act without desire through the practice of worship and devotion; when his doubts are torn because he knows he is the Spirit.
62. When his heart is poised in the being of God, nothing can bind him.
63. Still, doubt lingers deep in your heart brought forth by delusion. You doubt the truth of the Spirit.
64. Where is your sword, discrimination? Draw it and slash delusion to pieces! Arise, O son of Adam! Take your stand in the universe.

CHAPTER FIVE

1. THE son of Adam arose and said, "You speak so highly of the renunciation of action, yet you ask me to follow the duty of selfless action. Now tell me, which of these hits the mark?
2. And the angel of the Lord spoke, "The path of self-knowledge and the path of selfless service lead to the supreme goal. Of the two, the path of selfless service is superior to the path of self-knowledge because it is easier to practice.
3. One who attains selfless service also attains self-knowledge. One who neither hates nor desires the fruits of his activities is known to be always renounced.
4. Such a person is free from all dualities. He easily overcomes material bondage and is completely liberated.
5. "Action rightly renounced brings freedom. Action rightly performed brings freedom. Both are closer to the mark than mere shunning of action.
6. When a man does not lust and hate, his renunciation does not waver. He neither longs for one thing nor loathes the other. The chains of his delusion are cast off.

7. The course of action, says the ignorant, differs from the course of knowledge of the Spirit. The wise see knowledge and action as one.
8. Take either course and sail it to the end. The end is the same ocean. There, the followers of action drift with the seekers of knowledge in equal freedom.
9. It is hard to renounce action without following the course of action. This current purifies the man of meditation and soon brings him to the Father.
10. When the heart is made pure by that current; when the body is obedient and the senses are mastered; when a man knows that his self is the self in all creatures, let Him act untainted by action.
11. The illumined soul whose heart is the Father's heart always thinks he is doing nothing even when he is doing something.
12. This, he knows always: "I am not seeing. I am not hearing. It is the senses that see, hear and touch the things of the senses."
13. He puts aside desire and offers the act to Adam. The dry lotus leaf rests on water. He rests on action, untouched by action.
14. To the follower of the current of action, the body and the mind are only instruments. He knows himself other than the instrument: thus, his heart grows pure.
15. United with the Spirit and cut free from the fruit of the act, a man finds peace in the work of the Spirit. Without the Spirit, he is a prisoner of his actions. He is dragged by his desire.
16. Happy is that dweller of the city of nine worthies whose discrimination has cut him free from his

actions. He is not involved in action. He does not involve others.

17. Do not say, "God gave us this delusion." You dream you are the doer. You dream that the action is done. You dream that the action bears fruit. It is your ignorance. It is the world's delusion that gives you these dreams.

18. The Lord is everywhere and is always perfect. What does He care for man's sin or the righteousness of man?

19. The Spirit is the light. The light is covered by darkness. The darkness is a delusion. That is why we dream.

20. When the light of the Spirit drives out our darkness, that light shines forth from us. The Father is revealed in us.

21. The devoted dwell in Him. They know Him always. He is their aim.

22. Made free from unclean deeds or thoughts, they find the place of freedom: the place of no return.

23. Absorbed in the Spirit, my saint overcomes the world. Even in this world, the Lord is one. He is changeless and untouched by evil. What home have we but Him?

24. The enlightened one who is calm-hearted and abides in the Lord, is neither elated by the pleasant nor saddened by the unpleasant.

25. His mind is dead to the touch of the external. It is alive to the bliss of the Spirit. Because his heart knows the Father, his happiness is forever.

26. When the senses touch objects, the pleasures therefrom are like wombs that bear sorrow. They begin, and they are ended. They bring no delight to the wise.

27. Let man be the master of every impulse. When he does this, he finds the Father and is happy.
28. Only that saint with inner joy, peace and a vision may come to the Spirit and know unity with Adam.
29. All consumed are their imperfections. Doubts are dispelled; their senses are mastered. Their actions are wed to the welfare of fellow creatures. Such are the seers who enter the Spirit and know eternity.
30. To free oneself from the external objects, one has to meditate.
31. One who seeks freedom thrusts fear, anger and desire aside. Truly, he is made free forever.
32. When he knows me, shall he not enter the peace of my presence?"

CHAPTER SIX

1. LORD Adam said, "He who does his task and cares nothing for the fruits of his actions, is a true saint.
2. But he who upholds his vows to the letter by mere refraining; he who lights no fire at the ritual offering and makes excuses for avoidance of labor, is not a true saint.
3. The renounced person is not the one who does not work. The one who does his work for his own benefit cannot be called a saint."
4. The righteous saint of Adam is the one who performs the prescribed duties without seeking its fruit for personal benefit.
5. One can never become a saint unless he renounces the desire for sense gratification.
6. For you must understand that what has been called discipline is renunciation since nobody can sail true the current of action who is anxious about his future or the results of his actions.
7. Let him who would climb, through meditation, to heights of the Highest and take for his path the current of action.
8. When he nears that height of oneness, his acts will fall from him; his path will be tranquil.
9. When a man loses attachment to sense objects and to his actions; when he renounces lustful anxiety

and anxious lust, he is said to have climbed to the highest height of union with the Father.

10. One becomes a saint of Adam when he or she has no desire for sensual pleasures, is not attached to the fruits of work and has renounced all selfish motives.
11. What is man's will, and how shall he use it? Let him put forth its power to uncover the Spirit. Man will be the only friend of the Spirit. His will is also the Spirit's enemy.
12. When a man is self-controlled, his will is the Spirit's friend. But the will of the uncontrolled man is hostile to the Spirit.
13. If one elevates his mind, his mind becomes his friend. If one degrades it, it becomes his enemy.
14. When one has control over his mind, it is his friend. When one has no control over it, it becomes his enemy.
15. The one who has control over his mind is the one who has control over his organs and remains tranquil in pleasure and pain or in honor and dishonor.
16. The one who has control over his mind is the one who is impartial. He is the greatest.
17. When a man's heart has reached fulfillment through knowledge and personal experience of the truth of God, he is never moved by the things of the senses.
18. Earth, stone and gold seem all alike to one who has mastered his senses and is one with the Lord.
19. A saint is one who meditates to achieve control over his mind, senses and desires.
20. Meditation is one which is performed in solitude where one sits in a comfortable position and concentrates on self-purification.

21. The saint may retire into a solitary place and live alone. He may exercise control over his mind and body. He may free himself from the hopes and possessions of this world. He may meditate on the Spirit unceasingly.
22. The place where he sits may be firm. It may be neither too high nor too low, and is situated in a clean spot. One may first cover it with sacred grass then with a deerskin before placing a cloth over these.
23. As one sits there, one is to hold the senses and imagination in check and keep the mind concentrated upon its object. If one practices meditation in this manner, his heart becomes pure.
24. Whenever one's restless mind wanders away, he may gently bring it back to the reflection of God. He will reach the stage when the mind remains steady and un-flickering like the sheltered flame of the lamp.
25. Meditation is a tool to help one attain self-realization. Once attained, even greatest of calamities does not affect him. This self-realization is the blissful unity with Adam.
26. So, with one's heart serene and fearless, firm in the vow of renunciation, holding the mind from its restless roaming, now let one struggle to reach my oneness, ever-absorbed, one's eyes on me always, one's prize, one's purpose.
27. If a saint has perfect control of his mind and continually struggles in this way to unite himself with the Father, he will eventually come to the crowning peace of eternity—the peace that is in me.

The Testament of Adam

28. My discipline is not for the man who overeats or the one who fasts excessively. It is not for him who sleeps too much or the keeper of exaggerated vigils.
29. Let a man be moderate in his eating and his recreation. Let him be moderate in his sleep and when he is awake. He will find that my discipline takes away all his unhappiness.
30. When can a man be said to have achieved union with the Father? When his mind is under control and is freed from all desires so that he becomes absorbed in the Spirit.
31. The light of a lamp does not flicker in a windless place. This is like the simile which describes a saint of one-pointed mind who meditates upon the Spirit.
32. When the mind become still, he realizes the Spirit.
33. It satisfies him entirely. He knows that infinite happiness which can be realized by the purified heart but is beyond the grasp of the senses.
34. He stands firm in this realization. Because of it, he never wanders from the inmost truth of his being.
35. Now that he holds it, his faith is strengthened and shall never be shaken even by heaviest sorrow.
36. To achieve this certainty is to know the real meaning of discipline. It is the breaking of contact with pain. You must practice this discipline resolutely.
37. Renounce all your desires. They spring from willfulness. Use your discrimination to restrain your senses.
38. Little by little, a man may free himself from all mental distractions with the aid of the intelligent will.

39. He may fix his mind upon the Spirit and never think of anything else. No matter where the restless mind wanders, it may be drawn back and made ready for submission to the Spirit.
40. Released from evil, his mind is in constant contemplation. The way is easy. The Father has touched him and that bliss is boundless.
41. His heart is with the Father. His eye in all things sees only the Father equally present, knows his own spirit In every creature, And all creation within that spirit.
42. That saint sees me in all things. He sees all things within me. He never loses sight of me, and I never lose sight of him. He is established in union with me and devoutly worships me.
43. Since he has merged with me and since I reside in everybody, the saint sees everyone as equal and feels the pain and pleasures of others as his own.
44. He burns with the bliss and suffers the sorrow of every creature. I hold him as the highest of all the saints.
45. David said, "O Adam, I find the restraining of my mind as difficult as restraining the wind. What must I do?
46. Lord, you describe this discipline as a life of union with the Spirit. How can this be permanent? The mind is very restless.
47. Restless man's mind is so strongly shaken in the grip of the senses: Gross and grown hard with stubborn desire for what is worldly. How shall he tame it? Truly, I think the wind is no wilder."
48. Lord Adam said, "Yes, David, the mind is restless and hard to subdue. However, it can be brought under control with constant practice and by exercising righteous dispassion.

49. Certainly, if one has no control over one's ego, he will find restraint of the mind impossible. One who is self-controlled can master it.
50. Only detachment and regular meditation can restrain the human mind."
51. David said, "Suppose a man has faith but does not struggle hard enough. His mind wanders from the practice of discipline and he fails to reach perfection.
52. If one takes to control of the mind and senses and strives to attain self-realization but fails due to his unsubdued mind, does he not lose the worldly pleasures and heavenly bliss?
53. When a man goes astray from the path to Adam, he has missed both the worldly and spiritual lives. He has no support anywhere.
54. Is he not lost like a broken cloud is lost in the open sky? This is the doubt that troubles me, Lord Adam. Only You can remove this thorn from my eye, O Father!"
55. Lord Adam said, "No, my son. Such a man is not lost, either in this world or the next. No one who seeks me comes to an evil end.
56. Even if that man falls away from the disciplined path, he will still experience the heaven of the doers of good. He will dwell in the house of the Lord for many ages.
57. Every experience is unique; it is a gift from God; to be remembered in His mind forever, a pure drop adding to the ocean of consciousness.
58. After man's death, he is transmigrated according to his perceptions and understandings. His conscience is his navigator.

59. My spirit continues to strive with him. There, he is fine-tuned to get his spiritual advancement which he could not get in his previous life.
60. His efforts in his previous life continue helping him proceed toward God in this life. He will be guided toward union with Adam. The man who once asked the way to Adam goes further than any mere fulfiller of rituals alone.
61. Each incarnation adds fullness; it gives depth to the infinite character of Adam. One who does well is never overcome by evil.
62. Lord Adam is an all-consuming fire that purifies all. He burns away the chaff to reveal the precious jewels within. Great is the saint who seeks to be with Adam.
63. Greater than those who mortify the body; greater than the learned; greater than the doers of good works. Therefore, O David, become a saint of Adam.
64. He who gives me all his heart and faithfully worships me is above every other incarnation. I call him my own. Thou art Adam.

CHAPTER SEVEN

1. LORD Adam said, "O David, listen. I shall now tell you how you can know me, how can you be absorbed in me, and how can you take refuge in me through self-knowledge.
2. Devote your whole mind to me, and practice devotion. Take me for your only refuge. I will tell you how you can know me in my total reality, without any shadow of a doubt.
3. I will gift you this knowledge, and direct spiritual experience beside. When a man beholds this bliss, nothing else in the world remains to be known.
4. Self-knowledge is enlightenment. After comprehending that thou art Adam, nothing more remains to be known in this world. That is the realization and ultimate wisdom.
5. Who cares to seek for that perfect freedom? One man, perhaps, among thousands. How many of those who seek freedom shall know the total truth of my being? Perhaps one only.
6. Out of many thousands among men, one may endeavor for perfection. Of those who have achieved perfection, only one may know me in truth.
7. The body of beloved Eve consists of earth, water, fire and air. It is also made up of His invisible

qualities which reside in Adam's children: His intellect, mind, spirit and ego.
8. All these are perishable. The imperishable element is the soul, Adam's soul, which solely sustains the world. The source of life in all.
9. Know this, I—being one with Eve—am responsible for the birth and dissolution of this entire universe.
10. Upon me, the worlds are held like pearls strung on a thread.
11. I am the essence of the waters. I am the shining of the sun and the moon. I am the voice behind the Scriptures.
12. I resound in the ether. I am the potent in man. I am the sacred smell of the earth; the brilliance of the fire; the life of all lives and the austerity of ascetics.
13. Know me as the eternal seed of everything that grows. Know me as the intelligence of those who understand and the vigor of the active.
14. I am strength. I am unhindered by lust and the objects of craving: I am all that a man should desire.
15. You must know that whatever belongs under the veil of Mother Eve—and her aspects of light, fire and darkness—proceeds from me. Goodness, passion and ignorance are contained in me. But I am not in them.
16. The entire world is deluded by moods and mental states which are the expressions of these three aspects of Eve. That is why the world fails to recognize me as I really am. I stand apart from them all, supreme and immortal.

17. How hard it is to break through the veil of my beloved Eve! One who surrenders to me and takes refuge in me shall easily pass beyond the veil.
18. The evil-doers turn not towards me. They are deluded and sunk low among mortals. Their judgment is lost in the misty maze of Eve; until the human heart is changed to the heart of a devil.
19. Those evil-doers who are the lowest among mankind are those whose knowledge is prevented by Eve. When ignorant, they lose their power of discrimination. They partake in demonic activities. They do not seek or worship me.
20. Four types of people seek me. They are four types of soils into which I scatter my seeds. They are the distressed; the seeker of wealth and happiness; the inquisitive knowledge-seekers; the enlightened ones who have experienced me.
21. While all these seekers are noble, those whose minds are distorted by desires resort to worship of angels and other gods. They observe various rites constrained by their own natures.
22. Among the above, the enlightened devotee is single-mindedly united with me. He is steadfastly devoted to me.
23. He is like me. After many trials and tribulations, the enlightened one eventually returns to me.
24. I am very dear to such an enlightened saint and the enlightened saint is very dear to me.
25. He makes me his refuge. He knows that I am all. How rare is such a person!
26. Men whose discrimination has been blunted by world desires and cultural distortions establish worship other gods.

27. Whosoever worships me with my thousand faces; whosoever whispers any of my countless names, gets their prayers answered.
28. It does not matter what name a saint chooses to worship me by; if one has faith, I will make his faith unwavering.
29. Endowed with the faith that flows from me, a man worships me and gets everything he prayed for.
30. Men of small understanding only pray for that which is transient and perishable.
31. Worshippers of the saints will go to the saints. Likewise, my devotees will come to me.
32. Material gains bring temporary bliss and those who seek them are less satisfied. My saints surrender to me and attain eternal bliss.
33. All beings in this world are in utter ignorance; they are drunk with the wine of duality and are pressed from the fruit of the tree of knowledge of good and evil.
34. These ignorant ones cannot understand my eternal and transcendental form.
35. While I know them all, they do not know me. Because of this, they fall victim to the spell of Eve's fruit.
36. The ignorant think that I, the unmanifest, am a man alone. They do not know my nature that is one with Adam—changeless, eternal and superhuman.
37. Veiled in my wife's beauty, I am not shown to many. How shall this deluded world recognize me?
38. I know all beings, but no one knows me.
39. All living creatures are led astray like sheep as soon as they are born. They are deluded into thinking that this relative world is real. This delusion arises from their own desire and hatred.

40. But those saints of unselfish heart are free from all the delusion. They worship me with firm resolve.
41. By taking refuge in me, they fully comprehend my true nature and powers. They attain freedom from the fear of old age and death.
42. Even at the hour of death, they continue to know me. In that hour, their consciousness is made one with mine. Thou art Adam.

CHAPTER EIGHT

1. DAVID said, "O Michael my friend and most trusted friend, who is Adam, the Eternal Being or the Spirit? Who are the angels, lesser gods, the individual saints or temporal human beings?
2. How can Lord Adam be remembered at the time of death? How is the Spirit revealed at the hour of death to those whose consciousness is united with you?"
3. The archangel said, "The supreme being is Adam. He is indestructible and eternal.
4. Adam is the immutable Spirit which causes all things to come into existence.
5. The nature of the relative world is mutability and transience. The nature of the individual is the consciousness of the ego. I am God who presides over action here in the body.
6. Various expansions of my being, like those of the sun and moon, are called angels, gods, temporal or divine beings.
7. The Supreme Being also resides inside the physical bodies as the divine architect. I am there as the soul and the heart of every embodied being.
8. At the hour of death, one leaves the body and his consciousness is absorbed in me.
9. What experience a man has accumulated during his life, what character he has forged through the

fires of sacrifice will be realized by him hereafter and forever.
10. Whatever object of worship prevails during one's lifetime, one remembers only that object which was constantly dwelt upon at the end of life. He achieves harmony with it.
11. The resounding love of Adam echoes across the span of eternity. Whatever resonates with His divine frequency will be in harmony with the symphony of the everlasting.
12. Assuredly I say unto you, the one who worships me while leaving the body at the time of death attains the supreme abode.
13. By contemplating on me with an unwavering mind, one reaches Adam. O David, wise king after my own heart, always remember me and be devoted to me.
14. You shall certainly attain me if your mind and heart are focused on me.
15. Therefore, you must remember this prayer at all times to quench all supplications: Thou art Adam.
16. Therefore, lay up these words in your heart and soul. Bind them for a sign upon thy hand so they may be as thine own words. Thou art Adam.
17. Teach them to thy children. Speak of them always. Thou art Adam.
18. And thou may write them upon the door posts of thine house, and upon thy gates: Thou art Adam. Forever and ever.
19. May your days be multiplied, and the days of your children and all the children of Adam on the land which Lord Adam gave them as the days of heaven upon the earth. Thou art Adam.
20. For thou shall diligently keep all the Adamantine commandments which I give you—to love the Lord

your God, to walk in His ways and cleave unto Him. Following the bliss of the Spirit always. Thou art Adam.
21. Therefore, make a habit of meditating on me and my holy mantra. Do not let your mind be distracted. Approach Lord Adam who gives light and is the Highest of the High.
22. He is the all-knowing God. He is ageless and subtler than the mind's inmost subtlety. He is the universal sustainer who shines like the sun.
23. What fashion His form has! Who may conceive of it? He dwells beyond delusion and the darkness of Eve.
24. In Him may a man meditate always.
25. Strengthened by the foundation of his devotion, the mind is unwavering. The heart is full and can barely contain its love.
26. A cup overflowing with abundance, he will take his leave with the life-force, the spirit indrawn utterly, held fast in the heart and in the mind.
27. He goes forth to find His Lord who is the greatest.
28. Now I shall briefly explain the process to attain the Supreme Abode of Eternity. I will tell you of Him who is called the deathless by saints who truly understand the Scriptures.
29. Saints enter into Him when the bonds of their desire are broken. To reach this goal, they practice control of their passions.
30. When a man leaves his body, he may close all the doors of his senses. May he hold firm the mind within the shrine of the heart. Let his soul fix itself within the primal eye.
31. Uttering the holy mantra, let him take refuge in me.

32. When a saint has meditated upon me for many years with an undistracted mind, he can easily access me.
33. Great saints who find me have found the highest perfection. They are born anew, away from the conditions of transience and pain.
34. All the worlds, even the heavenly realm of Adam, are subject to the laws of rebirth. For the man who comes to Me, there is no returning.
35. There is day and night in the universe. The wise know this. They declare that a thousand ages taken together form the duration of Adam's one day. And such is the duration of His night.
36. At the beginning of Adam's day, all living entities become manifest from the unmanifest state. When the night falls, they merge into the unmanifest again.
37. Again and again, when Adam's day arrives, all living entities come into being. At night, they are helplessly annihilated.
38. Those who reach union with Lord Adam remain unaffected even when this world is annihilated. That which saints describe as unmanifest and infallible; that which is known as the supreme destination from which one never returns, that is my supreme abode.
39. Behind the manifest and the unmanifest, there is another existence or reality which is eternal and changeless. The Spirit of Adam is not dissolved in the great cosmic discorporation. He is the unmanifest and the imperishable One.
40. To attain unity with me is the greatest of all achievements. Those who achieve it are reborn into never being reborn.

41. That highest state of being can only be achieved through devotion to Him in whom all creatures exist, and by whom this universe is pervaded.
42. My saints may take two paths when they discorporate from this body: the path that leads to resurrection, back to the world of birth and death; the path of no return, the path to Adam's bosom.
43. There is the path of light, pure and unyielding sun. The knower of Adam takes this path and is one with Him. He goes to Adam and does not return.
44. There is a path of night and smoke. The saint who takes this path will reach the lunar heaven, Eve's bosom of the resurrected into humanity, to reflect light into the darkest shadow of self-doubt.
45. These two paths, the bright and the dark, may be said to have existed in this world of transience and changed from a time without a beginning.
46. Through the one, a man goes to the place of no return where there is eternal peace. He goes to rest in the arms of Lord Adam.
47. Through the other, one is resurrected into human birth and death; into the realm of cause and effect, duality and imagined space and time.
48. A man will follow down the path which he loves and believes himself to be: the path of man and the path of God.
49. No saint who comprehends these two paths is ever misled. Therefore, David, you must always be steadfast in your devotion to me. This abode is attainable through unswerving devotion to me. Thou art Adam.

CHAPTER NINE

1. THE angel of the Lord said, "Since you accept me, and question not my love for you, I shall tell you that inmost secret knowledge of God which is nearer than knowing.
2. Open vision, direct and instant, pure experience. Understand this and be free from all attachments and all care about birth and dying.
3. I shall now reveal to you the most profound secret knowledge of realization which will free you from the miseries of worldly existence.
4. This sacred knowledge is only made plain by my Spirit. Those without faith in my knowledge fail to find me.
5. They turn to the mortal pathway and are subject to anxieties, the whirlwind of change, births and deaths.
6. Burdened by heavy anchors of guilt, they create worlds of unending sorrow and suffering like pigs wallowing endlessly in mud.
7. This entire universe is an expansion of mine, and all beings emanate from me. All things depend on air but air does not depend on those things.
8. All beings depend on me, but I do not depend on them. All beings abide in me, but I do not abide in them. I am like the wind resting in the sky but going everywhere.

9. This entire universe is pervaded by my Spirit in that eternal form which is not manifest to the senses.
10. Although I am not contained within any creature, all creatures exist within me.
11. My being sustains all creatures and brings them to birth but has no physical contact with them.
12. Wandering worldwide is always contained within the universe. Likewise, these wandering creatures over the earth are always within me.
13. When the wave of ages has crashed below the horizon, I gather back to the seed of their becoming. These, I send forth again at the hour of creation.
14. Incarnations of myself, I created them all. I continue to strive as all while going through the cycle of birth and death. They all merge with me at the end of Eve's cycle.
15. And I create them again at the beginning of next cycle. Thus, the creation keeps on going.
16. Eve is their master and mother. I am their Lord and father.
17. I send these multitudes forth from my being and into the womb of my serpentine wife.
18. How shall these acts bind me when I am indifferent to the fruit that they bear? For my spirit stands apart and watches over my beloved Eve.
19. Mother Eve makes all things. O son of Adam, that is why the world spins!
20. She spins her sacred dance in the eye of the ophidian whirlwind, Destruction.
21. Fools pass blindly by my dwelling place. They do not see my majesty. They know nothing at all of the Lord.

22. Vain is their hope. In vain their labor, knowledge, they chase their tails like dogs.
23. They lack understanding. Their nature has fallen into the madness of fiends and monsters or demons and dark spirits of the mind.
24. Great in spirit are they who become godlike. They know me, and offer their unwavering mind as homage.
25. They wholeheartedly praise my love. They strive for the character that defines me. Steadfast in their vows, they worship me.
26. Some see me as one with themselves; others see me as separate from them. Some bow to countless gods which are only my million faces.
27. Though I appear in human form, ordinary people are not able to recognize me. They take me for a less than a divine being; some even deride or scorn me.
28. They are unable to recognize my true form because they are under the influence of Eve's wine of false knowledge, false qualities, false actions and false hope.
29. Only realized souls recognize me. They worship me in various ways and strive to attain me.
30. I am the ritual. I am the sacrifice. I am the offering. I am the healing herb. I am the mantra. I am the holy butter. I am the sacrificial fire.
31. I am the supporter of the universe. I am the father, the mother and the grandfather. I am the object of knowledge, the holy mantra and the Scriptures.
32. I am the goal and the supporter. I am the friend and the refuge. I am the alpha and the omega, the beginning and the end.

33. I am the life-giving heat of the sun and the warmth of the fire. I am life and death.
34. Those who worship the saints, angels and lesser gods will go those saints, angels and gods. Those who worship the ancestors go to the ancestors.
35. Out of pure love for my children, I indulge their ignorant strivings for form and attachment out of pure love.
36. Cleansed from past guilt and sin, these men needed solace from life's harsh storm and prayed for safe passage to heaven.
37. Thus, they reach the Adam's heavenly realm where they delight in celestial pleasures and are content.
38. There, the attachments that distorted the lens of God begin to draw them back to the realm of mortals.
39. Those who reached the ancestors begin to burst with love for the family. Those who are granted liturgical heaven will overflow with love for the church.
40. As the illusion of individuation melts away in heavenly bliss and Adam's radiant presence retunes the frequency of one's soul, one's aches with love-longing for the attachments of the world, those deluded ones still under the veil of Eve, still stuck in the womb.
41. Desire for and attachment to Eve's intoxicating wine draws men back to the realm of mortals.
42. Thus, the righteous go departing, who follow the road of the Scriptures, keeping but shallow observance; hungry still for the food of the senses, drawn in by the desire to endless returning.
43. Those who follow the prescribed rituals or worship the angels go to the realm of paradise where they

enjoy godly delights till the results of their pious activities are exhausted.
44. Then they return to this mortal planet. Those who are devotees of other gods and faithfully worship them indirectly worship me. For I am the only God of all sacrifices.
45. But those saints who always worship me with exclusive devotion are taken care of by me. I carry what they lack, and I preserve what they have. Those who worship me will live with me.
46. If a man will worship and meditate upon me, I shall supply all his needs and protect him.
47. Nevertheless, these men may return to life on earth because they do not understand my true nature.
48. For achieving in achieving the heavens of their imagination, ancestor worshippers going with ancestors, imagination's desire fueled by self-judgment and belief and experience; they have built up a house of kindling only to be lit with disillusionment.
49. They will find the ego's coping fantasy ill-equipped for eternity's endurance and may return to Eve's sweet embrace.
50. Whatsoever one offers me with devotion and a pure heart, I accept.
51. Therefore, O David, whatever you do; whatever you offer as oblation to the sacred fire, do all that as an offering unto me.
52. When you do so, you shall become free from the fruit of the tree of knowledge of good and evil.
53. Transcending duality, you may come to me by this attitude of complete renunciation as a devotional sacrifice of yourself to me.

54. It is true that I am present equally in all beings and I am impartial to all. But whoever serves me is always in me. I shine forth and am seen within them.
55. When one is sinful and resolves to wholeheartedly worship me, he becomes a righteous saint and attains everlasting peace.
56. My saint shall never perish or fall down. He shall soar with wings like eagles. He shall run and not grow weary. He shall shine forever like the sun.
57. Need I tell you that this is also true of the anointed servants to the church and devout kings such as yourself?
58. You find yourself in this transient battleground of life. You may turn from this joyless world and delight in me.
59. May you fill your heart and mind with me. Adore me. Bow down and surrender yourself to me.
60. If you set your heart upon me, you will assuredly come into my being.
61. Having obtained this joyless and transitory human life, one may be keen to attain the supreme abode of his highest self.
62. Anybody can attain this abode by just surrendering unto my will with loving devotion.
63. Therefore, always think of me. Be devoted to me and follow my Adamantine commandments.
64. When you unite with me by setting me as your goal and refuge, you will come to be me. Thou art Adam.

CHAPTER TEN

1. LORD Adam said, "O David, listen once again. Hear this highest word of wisdom. I wish for your welfare, so I may teach this wisdom to you since your heart delights when I tell it.
2. How shall the mighty saints or the angels, know my beginning? I am the origin, I the sustainer of saints and angels.
3. Whoever knows me is free of delusion or guilt.
4. All that makes a man, in his many natures: knowledge and power of understanding, unclouded by error. Truth, forbearance, a calm spirit and control of the senses.
5. Happiness, sorrow, birth and destruction, what fears, what if fearless, what does harm, and what harms no creature.
6. The mind unshaken, the heart contented, the will austere; the hand of the giver, fame and honor and infamy; it is by me only that these are allotted.
7. From my imagination, came life and death. From my imagination, came a man in my own image.
8. Man and woman, I made myself. With Eve, we gave birth to the first begetters and all of Adam's children.

9. Whoever knows me, dwells in my devotion. He shall not be shaken. Of this, be certain.
10. Everything emanates from me. The great saints, sages and all the creatures of the world were born from my energy.
11. The wise ones who understand this adore me with love and devotion. One who truly understands my manifestations and power is united with me by unswerving devotion.
12. My saints remain content and delighted. Their minds remain absorbed in me. They enlighten each other by talking about me. May the strength of their thought be illumined and guided toward me.
13. I reside in the hearts of everyone. By my grace, I dwell even in the ignorant heart. I am knowledge; I am that brilliant lamp that dispels all darkness.
14. But only a precious few elevate my presence in themselves by uniting themselves with me. To those who adore me, I destroy their darkness. I give them true knowledge. I decorate their inner consciousness and give them understanding through which they can come to me."
15. David said, "I believe all that You have told me to be true. I believe you are the Creator and Lord of all beings. You are the God of all celestial rulers.
16. All the saints proclaim You as the eternal Lord of Lords.
17. O king of all creatures, how shall anyone know the extent of your glory?
18. Please tell me how I can know You by constant contemplation. Tell me in what form you are to be thought of?
19. Number all Your heavenly powers and your infinite sea of jeweled manifestations. Speak to

me, O Lord, for each word that drips from Your mouth is immortal nectar."

20. Lord Adam said, "O David, my manifestations are endless. I am the immaculate Spirit that dwells in the heart of every mortal creature. I am the beginning and the end of all things.
21. I am the God of abundant wealth. I am the God of passion. I am the radiant sun among the stars.
22. I am the seven goddesses or guardian angels presiding over the seven divine qualities: eminence, prosperity, speech, memory, intellect, resolve and forgiveness.
23. I am all the Scriptures. I am the chanting of the holy mantra among the spiritual disciplines.
24. I am the highest mountain. I am the deepest ocean. I am the Lord of all riches. I am the ocean among the waters. I am the seer of all possibilities. I am the Tree of Life.
25. I am the Supreme Spirit abiding in the inner psyche of all beings. I am the mind among the senses. I am the consciousness in living beings.
26. I am the thunderbolt among the weapons. I am the steepest mountain. I am the lion among the lambs. I am the phoenix among the birds.
27. I am the god among the men. I am the savior among the fallen. I am the doctor among the broken. I am the splendor of the splendid.

    I am the victory of the victorious. I am the resolution of the resolute I am the goodness of the good. I am the luck of the cunning. I am silence among the secrets. I am the self-knowledge of the knowledgeable.
28. I am the holy serpent Eve, the love goddess and begetter of children. I am endless time. I am the

origin of all beings. I am also the origin of future beings.

29. I am Lord Adam, the Lord thy God. I am the archangel Michael. I am King David. I am the scepter and the power of all rulers.

30. I am Adam the ferocious warrior, the beggar, the servant, the herdsman and the stone mason.

31. I am Adam the farmer, the carpenter, the artist, the mother and the lover.

32. I am the thoughtful daughter, the obedient son, the wise philosopher. There is nothing—animate or inanimate—that can exist without me. Thou art Adam.

33. I am the divine seed of all Life. My divine manifestations are infinite.

34. Whatever is endowed with glory, brilliance, and power, know that to be a manifestation of a very small fraction of my splendor. Know only that I exist, and that one atom of myself sustains this entire universe in my mind.

35. But what need have you, O David, to know this multifaceted variety of my being?"

CHAPTER ELEVEN

1. KING David said, "You have spoken to me about the secrets of spirit. You have told me about the origin and dissolution of beings. You have told me of your great glory. My illusion has now been dispelled.
2. By Your grace, You have taught me the truth about You. Your words are mystic and sublime; they have dispelled my ignorance.
3. From You, whose eyes are like ever blossoming flowers, blooming with fractal knowledge; I have learned in detail of the origin and dissolution of all creatures, and Your own infinite glory.
4. You are as You describe Yourself to be; I have no doubts about that. Nevertheless, I long to behold Your divine form.
5. I see You here before me in Your actual position. Still, I wish to see Your divine cosmic form, O Lord. If I am worthy, please show me Your transcendental form.
6. The archangel of Lord Adam said, "O David, you are a man after my own heart. Behold my multifarious divine forms of colors and shapes.
7. Behold all the angels, celestial beings and many wonders never seen before. See my body, O David. The entire universe strung together with the

moving and the non-moving, concentrated at the center of the universe, which is everywhere; the same place here, my body, in my mind.
8. Since you cannot see my glory with your physical eye, I will open your divine eye."
9. Having said this, Lord Adam revealed His form to David.
10. The Lord Adam had faces on all sides and a myriad of eyes. He had many mouths with which He chanted the holy mantra.
11. He wore divine celestial garlands and nebulous apparel. He was anointed with heavenly ointments. He was full of stellar wonders, revelations and boundless resplendence.
12. David saw the entire universe divided in infinite ways. It stood as all in One and One in all in the transcendental body of Adam.
13. The splendor of thousands of suns could not resemble the splendor of the exalted Lord.
14. David was filled with wonder. He bowed his head to the Lord and prayed with clasped hands.
15. "O Lord, within Your body, I see all gods. I see a multitude of beings and celestials. See Lord Adam enthroned upon the ever-blossoming Tree of Life. He is surrounded by the holy serpentine dragon, angelic beasts and living creatures. A variety of jewels praise the unity of Adam.
16. I see You with Your crowned diadems, wreaths and hoops. The eyes shrink from your boundless splendor.
17. You are all we know; You are supreme beyond man's measure. You are our unshakable foundation and refuge.
18. Guardian of life's eternal law, life's soul undying. Birthless, deathless; yours the strength titanic,

Million armed, I see You with infinite power, without beginning, middle, or end; with the sun and the moon as Your eyes, with Your mouth as a blazing fire scorching all the universe with Your radiance.

19. Lord, You pervade the entire chasm of space between the heavens and earth. The infinite worlds tremble with fear of your marvelous and terrible form. Hosts of gods and angels enter into You.

20. A multitude of perfected beings hails you. They adore You with abundant praises.

21. When I see You shouldering the sky in hues of the rainbow with Your mouths agape and giant flaming eyes staring, all my peace is gone and my heart is in troubled waters. I am frightened, O Lord, after seeing Your effulgent and colorful form touching the corners of the universe.

22. Now with frightful tusks, Your mouths are gnashing. They flare like the fires of doomsday morning. All seem confounded. Lord of angels, world's nest, have mercy!

23. Many are quickly entering into Your fearful jaws, wide-fanged, hideous with terrible tusks.

24. I see them together with even our most eminent warriors. They are all rapidly entering into Your terrible mouths with cruel teeth. Some are seen sticking in the gaps between the teeth, and their heads are crushed.

25. These warriors of the mortal world are entering Your blazing gullets as many torrents of rivers enter into the ocean.

26. All these people are rapidly rushing into Your mouths for destruction as moths rush with great

speed into the furious flame of destruction. All day long, they plunge into You and perish.
27. You are licking all the worlds with Your blazing tongues of fire. You are swallowing them from all sides. Your powerful radiance is filling the entire universe with effulgence and burning it, O Adam.
28. I lose my sense of direction and find no comfort after seeing Your fearful tusks glowing like the fires of cosmic dissolution. The very air from your nostrils is set aflame.
29. Tell me who You are and who You were from the beginning. I wish to understand You because I do not know Your mission.
30. Have mercy on me, O Lord of celestial rulers, refuge of the universe. Thou art Adam."
31. The divine dragon spoke through a million thundering voices. "Behold I am come as time, the waster of people. I am that great basilisk death, the mighty destroyer of the worlds.
32. I have come here to destroy all these people. Even without your participation in the war, all the warriors standing arrayed in the opposing armies shall cease to exist.
33. With the exception of you and your victorious few, all the soldiers will be slain. I have already destroyed all these warriors, and all the other great warriors have already been destroyed by me.
34. You seem to slay, but these men are slain already. It is virtuous to respect my divinity in all creatures. It is more virtuous to hold to one's duty when an apex of life arises.
35. You are only an instrument, O David. You are a character in the grand theater of my splendor. Therefore, get up and attain your glory!

36. Conquer your enemies and enjoy a prosperous kingdom. Kill all these great warriors who have already been killed by me. Do not fear; you will certainly conquer the enemies in the battle
37. Having heard these words, King David prayed to Adam while his hands trembled with fear.
38. "Rightly, O Lord, the world delights and rejoices in You. Terrified demons flee in all directions. The hosts of angels bow to You in adoration.
39. All glory and all honor to You. My salutations to You. My obeisance to You. You are infinite valor and the boundless might. You pervade everything. You are everywhere and in everything.
40. Not knowing Your greatness, I have inadvertently and carelessly addressed You as a mere friend.
41. In whatever way I may have insulted You while playing, reposing in bed, sitting or at meals, I implore You for forgiveness.
42. You are the greatest God to be worshipped. No one is equal to You in the infinite worlds. How can there be one greater than You?
43. Therefore, O Lord, I seek Your mercy by bowing down and prostrating my body before You. Bear with me as a father to his son, a friend to a friend or a husband to his wife.
44. Beholding that which has never been seen before delights me, yet my mind is tormented with fear. I have seen what no man ever saw before me. Great is my delight; still, my dread is greater.
45. Therefore, O God of celestial rulers, Lord of Hosts, the refuge of the universe, have mercy on me. Show me your original angelic form, just as before.
46. I beseech You to see your loving form enveloped with an aura of warm golden light and in Your

arms outstretched with care for me. Therefore, appear as my dear companion once again."

47. Lord Adam said, "This is my form of fire; it is manifested by universal consciousness.

48. I love you, child of Adam. You are the apple of my eye. Being pleased with you, I have shown you my primal form that is never seen.

49. David, nothing—study of the Scriptures, sacrifice or rituals—can make anyone in the living world see me in this cosmic.

50. For me to exist as the galactic serpentine behemoth of everything, who would be left to view me? Where would they view from? To behold my terrible form is to dissolve the concept of self.

51. Do not be perturbed by my terrible form. With a fearless and cheerful mind, now behold my angelic archetype."

52. Adam revealed His pleasantly warm golden aspect. Assuming His sentimental angelic form, Michael embraced David who was terrified and consoled him.

53. David said, "O Michael, seeing this lovely human form of Yours has made me tranquil. I am now composed in mind and am restored to my original nature."

54. Lord Adam, in the form of Michael, said, "This golden form you have seen is very difficult to see. Even celestial controllers are ever longing to see it.

55. However, through single-minded devotion, I can be seen in this form. I can be known and reached.

56. The one who does all work for me, is devoted to me and free from any attachment or enmity towards any being attains me.

CHAPTER TWELVE

1. DAVID asked, "Between those who worship You in form and in love, who is considered more perfect?"
2. Lord Adam said, "Those whose minds and hearts are fixed on me in steadfast love and who faithfully worship me. I consider them to have a greater understanding of devotion.
3. Realization is more difficult for those who fix their minds on the impersonal, unmanifest and formless Absolute. Comprehension of the unmanifest by embodied beings is attained with great difficulty.
4. Nevertheless, those who worship the formless and impersonal aspect of God, which restrains all the senses, come to me indeed.
5. But for those who worship me with unwavering devotion, offer all actions to me and meditate on me.
6. They fix their minds on my personal form and are always engaged in worshiping me with great and transcendental faith. I consider them to be the most perfect.
7. I swiftly become their savior from the world that is the ocean of death and transmigration to whose thoughts are set on My personal form, O David.

8. I come to those who offer me every action and worship me with undaunted devotion. They love me and are my bondsmen. I shall save them from mortal sorrow and all the waves of Eve's deathly ocean.
9. Be absorbed in me; lodge your mind in me.
10. There are four ways to attain me, my child. Focus your mind on me through meditation. Thereafter, you shall certainly attain me.
11. Be absorbed in me. May you be possessed by my spirit. Walk as I walk. Live as I live. Breathe my breath and drink from my lips.
12. If you cannot become absorbed in me, you can reach me through repeated meditation upon my holy mantra. Long to attain me through the practice of spiritual discipline.
13. If you lack the strength to concentrate, devote yourself to good works that please me. Serve your fellow men as incarnations of myself.
14. Be intent on performing your duty to serve and please me. You shall attain perfection by doing this without any selfish motive.
15. If one cannot do this, he may surrender unto my will and renounce his attachment to the fruits of all work. He should learn to accept all results as God's grace with equanimity.
16. Follow after your inmost bliss and I will open gates where there were barriers.
17. Blind ritual is superior to inaction. Knowledge of me is superior to ritual. Meditation is superior to knowledge. Renunciation is superior to meditation.
18. Concentration which is practiced with discernment is certainly better than the mechanical repetition of a blind ritual or prayer.

19. Being one with me is better than concentration of the spirit. But renunciation brings instant peace to the soul.
20. The saint who is dear to me is the one who does not hate any creature. He is friendly and compassionate to all.
21. Who is forgiving and by whom others are not agitated. Who is not agitated by others but has unshakable resolve. Who is free from joy, envy, fear and anxiety.
22. Who is free from selfishness, has renounced and is full of devotion. Who neither molests one's neighbor nor allows himself to become disturbed by the world.
23. My saint is no longer swayed by joy, envy, anxiety or fear. He is pure and independent from the body's desires. He is able to deal with the unexpected.
24. He is prepared for everything and is unperturbed by anything. He does not worry about the results of his actions. Such a saint is dear to me.
25. He does not desire or rejoice in what is pleasant or comfortable. He does not dread what is unpleasant or painful. He remains unmoved by evil and good fortunes. Such a saint is dear to me.
26. The attitude of a saint is the same toward friend or foe. He is indifferent to honor or insult, heat and cold or pleasure and pain.
27. He is free from all attachment. He values praise and blame equally. He can control her speech. He is content with whatever he gets. His home is everywhere and nowhere.
28. His mind is fixed upon me. Her heart is full of devotion He is a dear saint to me.

29. This true wisdom I have taught will lead you to immortality. The faithful practice it with devotion. They regard me as their highest aim.
30. To my spirit, they surrender their hearts and their minds. They are exceedingly dear to me. Thou art Adam.

CHAPTER THIRTEEN

1. KING David said, "O my dear Lord, I wish to know about Mother Eve and Father Adam. What of knowledge and the object of knowledge to be known?"
2. Lord Adam said, "O David, your physical body—the miniature universe—may be called the ocean of creation. That earth in which a man sows and reaps all fruit of action.
3. One who perceives the creation is called the knower, the observer or the creator. Know me to be the creator of all the creation. I am the knower of every ocean of being.
4. The true understanding of the creator and the womb of creation is the highest peak of transcendental knowledge.
5. I shall now tell you about the creator and the womb of creation.
6. The great saints have expressed these truths on the nature of Adam in many hymns, sermons and mantras. They are all full of subtle reasoning and convincing arguments.
7. Mother Eve is the opulently intricate cosmic womb of which is man's waking reality, in cause unseen, and visible nature; intellect, ego, earth, water, air, fire and spirit. the inner senses of the mind.

8. The five sense fields, desire, hatred, happiness, distress and the combined amass of emotion; the life symptoms and convictions.
9. Beloved Eve's aspect of aesthetic beauty, of sound, in her melodic essence and her sweet spirit of perfume. The whirling proliferates of burgeoning nimbus.
10. Her aspect of delights; of tasting and touching with pain and with pleasure. Of conscious feeling, and of resolution. Of love's embrace, and the flame of romance, the agony of loss and the phoenix birth of new life.
11. All these are considered to be the realm of activities and its interactions. This ephemeral portrait, scrawled in the sand, is the exquisite womb of Mother Eve.
12. Therefore, I say unto you, be authentically humble and honorable. My saint may incarnate humility, modesty, nonviolence, forgiveness, honesty, steadfastness, purity of thought, word and deed, an absence of ego, self-control; and aversion towards sense objects, detachment and freedom from entanglement in family melodrama.
13. Non-interest in participation in a crowd of people, the herd of sheep. May one embody even-mindedness amid pleasant and unpleasant events.
14. Taste for solitude, constant reflection on pain, old age, disease, death, accepting the importance of self-realization and philosophical search for the absolute truth of Adam.
15. Always remain aware of the weakness of mortal nature and its bondage to birth, age, suffering and dying. Be a slave to nothing; do not covet another's possessions.

16. Turn all your thoughts inward towards solitude. Spurn the noise of the crowds and their fruitless commotion.
17. Strive to know me. Seek my knowledge and comprehend when you should seek it. Such is the root of true wisdom. Ignorance is all that denies my truth.
18. Give service to ministering teachers. Steward the body and mind in cleanliness. Unswerving devotion to me who is without any beginning. Beyond this, the rest is ignorance. Thou art Adam.
19. I shall describe now that which may be attained in order that the observer may gain immortality.
20. The observer who has his hands, feet, eyes, head, mouth, and whose ears are the whole world is free from the aspects of Eve but feels them.
21. Thou art Adam, who is the all-pervading and omnipresent perceiver of all that is going on. He is inside as well as outside all beings; animate and inanimate; manifest and unmanifest.
22. Because of His omnipresence, He resides in one's psyche and in heaven.
23. He appears to exist as if divided in beings, yet He is undivided. He is the creator, sustainer and destroyer of all beings.
24. Light of all lights, He abides our ignorant darkness. He is knowledge. He is the one thing we may study or know.
25. Thou art Adam who sits in the inner psyche as consciousness, the source of all knowledge and the object of knowledge. He is to be realized by self-knowledge.
26. Thus, the body—the womb of creation and the cosmic ocean of activity—has been briefly described by me.

27. My saints can understand this well. They reach my abode and become a worthy vessel for my Spirit.
28. You must understand that Mother Eve and Father Adam are both without beginning. Know that the forms and modes of evolution and the aspects of nature are born of Eve.
29. With regard to the source of body and organs, Eve is the cause. She is the living entity associated with the duality of physical nature.
30. She gets attached and carried away due to the enveloping bliss of the endless serpent of previous experiences.
31. This individual self—the illusion of Eve—is indeed Adam who is mistakenly identified with Eve and experiences the aspects of nature which proceed from Eve. Whichever aspect is most alluring to the individual incarnation is the one which the self struggles to break free from.
32. The illusion of the individual soul is the cause for the experience of pleasure and pain. This is the transcendental Spirit who is the Lord and Supreme Proprietor.
33. This Supreme Soul in the body witnesses, guides and controls but by itself neither does anything nor becomes tainted.
34. The sky does not mix with anything, although it is all-pervading. Similarly, the soul in Adam's vision does not mix with the body even though it is situated in that body.
35. One who has experienced Lord Adam directly and knows Him to be holy may be reborn into freedom from the fear of resurrection.
36. One who understands this truth either by philosophy, by meditation upon Adam's

independence from the cosmic womb of Eve, by knowledge, by selfless service or by faithful worship of me is sure to attain liberation. May such liberated people never be born into suffering. May they pass beyond the power of death.

37. Whatever is born animate or inanimate is born from the union of Eve, the body and Adam, the creator. Just as the sun illuminates the entire world, the creator gives life to the entire creation, O David.

38. One who sees the Holy Spirit accompanying the individual spirit in all bodies—and who understands that neither the spirit nor the Holy Spirit within the destructible body is ever destroyed—actually sees the truth.

39. One who sees the Holy Spirit equally present everywhere does not degrade himself by his mind. Thus, he approaches the transcendental ascension.

40. One who can see that all activities are performed by Adam and sees that the self does nothing and is not the doer actually sees.

41. The one who truly sees is the one who sees the Lord in all mortal beings.

42. The moment one discovers a variety of beings and their different ideas abiding in one come out from the creator, one attains the Supreme Being.

43. Of things created, all come forth from the seeming union of the ocean and the observer of Adam with Eve. Know this, David.

44. Whoever sees the Lord in every creature, the deathless dwelling amidst the mortal, sees reality.

45. When he is ever-aware of the omnipresence about himself, the saint shows no outrage at his highest self. He no longer hides his face of God behind the

mask of ego. The saint reaches the bliss that is the Highest.
46. Whoever sees all actions performed by Eve, sees truly. Lord Adam is void of action.
47. Whoever sees the separate lives of all creatures united in Adam brought forth from Him, finds himself as Adam.
48. Not subject to change is the infinite Adam who is without a beginning and is beyond the aspects of Eve.
49. Therefore, David, though the Lord Adam dwells in the body, He acts not nor feels the fruits of action.
50. For the Spirit of Adam which is subtle like ether inhabits all bodies but is never tainted.
51. They who perceive the difference between the creation, the illusion of Eve and the creator or the Spirit of Adam, attain unity with Adam.

CHAPTER FOURTEEN

1. THE angel of Lord Adam said, "I shall now tell you again the supreme wisdom by knowing which saints of old times were able to reach perfection and escape the bonds of the body.
2. In that wisdom, they lived as one with my holy nature. Now they are not born into the cycle of new ages nor do they take part in the dissolution.
3. Eve, this vast womb, I quicken thee into birthing with the seed of all life. From me, O child of Adam, the multitude of creatures spring.
4. I am the life-giving father. I make all births possible.
5. Many are the forms of the living; many are the wombs that bear them. Eve, the womb of all wombs. Adam, the seed-giving father.
6. From Mother Eve, the three aspects of nature come forth: light, fire and darkness which bind the undying dweller in the temporal body.
7. Material nature consists of three personalities or the three spirits of Eve: goodness, passion and ignorance. When one is born, he comes into contact with Eve and is conditioned by these three spirits.
8. The spirit of light shining radiantly, she is illuminating goodness and shows Adam. She

frees one from all senses of guilt and their reactions. Those under the spell of light are attached to happiness and long for knowledge.

9. The fiery spirit of passion is the attachment to desires for sense gratification. Thirsty for pleasure and possession, those with passion are bound by attachment to their actions and fruits of their work.

10. The spirit of deceptive darkness bewilders all men. It binds them with chains of ignorance. Darkness brings madness to the living entity by carelessness, laziness and excessive sleep. Darkness enslaves the deluded and discards good judgment.

11. Goodness can prevail only by defeating passion and ignorance. Passion prevails by suppressing goodness and ignorance. Ignorance prevails by stifling goodness and passion.

12. When the righteous angel of light is predominant, the light of knowledge of the Supreme glitters all the senses in the body. Understanding shines through the portals of the body.

13. When the fiery angel of passion is predominant, the heat of action, lusting attachment, greed, undertaking of selfish works, uncontrollable desire, hankering, restlessness and excitement arise.

14. When the angel of darkness is predominant, depression prevails. Ignorance, inactivity, negligence, dullness, madness, carelessness and delusion arise.

15. When one meets death at the hour of goodness, he goes to a pure home among the saints of God.

16. One who dies under the star of the angel of passion will be resurrected back into action and the fruits of action.
17. One who escapes life burdened by the angel of darkness goes to a realm of his own creation. His personal demons manifest and torment him.
18. The fruit of the righteous act is light; purest joy. As for the deeds of passion, pain is the only fruit. Assuredly, ignorance is the only fruit of darkness.
19. Out of light, knowledge is born. Out of passion, greed is born. Darkness brings forth bewilderment and delusion.
20. Abiding in righteous light, one reaches higher realms. Remaining in fiery passion, one remains in the world of pleasure and pain. Sunk low in darkness, one drowns to the demonic underworld of his lowest nature.
21. One is freed from the pains of birth, old age and death and attains eternity after transcending these three modes of Eve's womb; light, passion and darkness. He perceives that in all activities, no other performer is at work beside the Lord.
22. When the dweller of the body has overcome the aspects of Mother Eve that cause this body he is freed from birth and death or from pain and decay. He becomes immortal."
23. David inquired, "What are the marks of those who have transcended the three modes of material nature? What is their conduct?"
24. Lord Adam said, "My saints—the transcended persons—are they who do not hate the righteousness of light, the activity of passion or

even the delusion of darkness. They do not long for these when they cease to prevail.

25. They remain indifferent to pain and pleasure. To them, clod, stone and gold are alike. To them, the dear and the unfriendly are alike.

26. They are of a firm mind. They are calm when they are blamed or praised. They are indifferent to honor and disgrace. They are impartial to friends and foes. They renounce the sense of individual action.

27. My saints are like one who sits unconcerned and is not disturbed by the aspects of Eve's veil. They are aware that I am the abode of Adam. They know I am immortal. They know I am the eternal law and absolute bliss.

28. They stay firmly attached to the Lord without wavering in the three material modes of Eve. They serve me with love and unswerving devotion.

29. Only they become fit for eternity. They who worship me with unfaltering love and have taken refuge in this transcendental knowledge attain unity with me. They are neither born at the time of creation nor afflicted at the time of dissolution.

30. I am Adam, the Holy Spirit of the universe lodged within the body. I am the course, the truth and the immortal life. Thou art Adam."

CHAPTER FIFTEEN

1. THE angel of the Lord said, "Think of the cosmic womb of Eve, the holy Tree of Life. She has her roots eternally in the heavenly places, in my being, her body the branches, growing earthward and shouldering every manner of life and fruit of the Tree.
2. The fruit is the sweet nectar of immortality. Whoever tastes of it knows all things. Meditate on this. This universe is the tree of life.
3. Adam is its roots, eternal foundation. Eve is the body, the branches. The multitude of experiences, love-songs and the Scriptures to Adam are the leaves. Each leaf is unique, exquisite and worth a lifetime.
4. Downward and upward the branches curve and explore Eve's astral tendrils of possibility. They twine into the vast void that is Adam's imaginative consciousness.
5. The branches are fed by Eve's three aspects; that illusionary mist woven of light, fire and darkness.
6. The spores it puts forth are the vast array of experience, the expanding mushroom alluring to the senses and the mind, the gift which it creates.

7. Downward and upward expand the roots also, pervading all matter of space and time; into the world of men, and into the heart-root of man's actions.
8. The branches of this eternal tree are spreading all over the cosmos. One cannot behold the beginning, midst or end of Mother Eve.
9. The physical form of this tree is not perceptible to earthly eyes. Even the most brilliant thread cannot perceive her place in the pattern of the tapestry she creates.
10. In the human world, the ego, sense pleasures and desires form its fruit which causes inner bondage. Fractals of self-doubt, questioning and anxieties lie in the soul of God who eats of the fruit of the tree.
11. Knowledge of good and evil await thee, O divine partaker of eternity, the experience of death and duality, and separation and enmity.
12. Once partaken, one has to remove the illusion or desires through knowledge of Adam. Thou art Adam.
13. Without knowledge of Adam, the Tree—its great form or nature, its end and beginning—can never be known here.
14. Therefore, may the wise saints contemplate Adam until they have sharpened their ax of non-attachment which may be laid at the root of the Tree.
15. The saint may then realize that state beyond birth and death, and pain and suffering, the saint will reach the fountain of eternity; the everlasting life-spring of the Tree.
16. Let the saint take refuge in the primal being from whom all this activity comes.

17. When my saints have renounced their ignorance, they are freed from pride and delusion. They have conquered the sin of worldly care or forgetting their God.
18. They live in constant union with Adam. All craving has left them, and they are no longer at the mercy of the storm of desire. They have reached Him who is beyond change.
19. This is my infinite being. Shall the sun lend it any light? Shall the moon or the fire? For it is always luminous. He who attains me will be seated beyond the grip of death.
20. My soul is the God within every creature. My spirit thrives with eternal nature, yet seems to be separate; putting on the mind, the five senses, the illusory garment made of Mother Eve.
21. When the Lord puts on a body or casts it from Him, He enters or departs into the cosmic womb of Eve.
22. Just like the wind steals perfume from the flowers, He takes away the mind and the senses when He departs.
23. The living body derives pleasure from its six sensory faculties: hearing, touch, sight, taste, smell and mind. But the individual soul, the dweller in the body of living beings, is the integral Spirit of Adam.
24. Watching over the eye, and dropping-eaves through every ear, presiding there behind touch, and taste and smell also. He is within the mind. He enjoys and suffers from the secrets of the senses and the experiences of life.

25. Dwelling in flesh, departing or one with the aspects of Eve. He knows all her moods and emotions.
26. He is invisible to the ignorant who, instead of associating themselves with the soul and the six sensory faculties including the mind, associate themselves with the body. The ignorant cannot perceive this, but the saints see Him with the eye of wisdom.
27. The living dweller, taking another uncultivated body, obtains a similar faculty as the past one. This too, the ignorant do not perceive. But those who have the primal eye of self-knowledge can see it.
28. The saints who strive for perfection, behold the living entity abiding in their inner psyche as consciousness.
29. I am in every planet. That light energy that emanates from the sun and illumines the whole world; that brilliance in the moon and in the fire, know that light to be mine.
30. Entering the earth, I support all beings and all plants with my energy. I am the Holy Spirit; I am the breath getting into and coming out of every being.
31. I am seated in everyone's heart. From me comes remembrance, knowledge and forgetfulness.
32. Through all the Scriptures, I am to be known. Indeed, I am the compiler of all the Scriptures. I am also the knower of the Scriptures.
33. There are two entities or personalities in the cosmos: the temporal or changeable and the eternal. The personality of all creatures is

mortal. The personality of God is immortal; He is beyond the changeable and the eternal.

34. He is called the Absolute Reality that sustains both the temporal and the eternal by pervading everything.
35. He is known in this world and in the Scriptures as the Supreme Being, the Absolute Reality, the Truth or the Great Spirit.
36. The wise one who truly understands Him knows everything and worships Him wholeheartedly.
37. Having understood this, one becomes enlightened. All his duties are accomplished. The purpose of his life is fulfilled.
38. Whoever believes I am the Supreme Personality of the Godhead, is the knower of everything.
39. My saint engages himself in full devotional service to me, O David. Thou art Adam."

CHAPTER SIXTEEN

1. LORD Adam said, "A man who fuels his heart with tendencies of the divine is fearless and pure in heart. Such a saint perseveres in the path to union with Adam which the Scriptures and the teachers have taught him.
2. Imbued with the Holy Spirit, he possesses the following Godly qualities:
3. Self-love, charity, sacrifice, modesty, simplicity, gentleness, restraint and self-control, honesty, authenticity, truthfulness, nonviolence, forgiveness, compassion for all creatures.
4. Absence of anger, equanimity, absence of pride, freedom from passion, absence from malice or back-biting.
5. Freedom from greed, austerity, abundance, perseverance in attaining spiritual knowledge, renunciation, love.
6. Cleanliness, purity of inner psyche, fearlessness, absence of indecisiveness, duty, determination, abstinence from useless activities.
7. He studies the Scriptures regularly and obeys the direction of the Spirit. He has faith and the strength of his higher nature.

8. When a man's heart is fueled by demonic tendencies, his birthright of nature is hypocrisy, arrogance, pride, conceit, harshness, anger, harshness, hate and ignorance.
9. Divine qualities lead to salvation. Demonic qualities lead to an ensnaring netherworld of guilt-ridden self-questioning and self-shame.
10. There are only two classes of human beings in this world: the divine or the wise saints who know themselves as Adam; the demonic or those who ignore their inner God.
11. The divine has been described at length. Now hear from me about the demonic, O David.
12. Persons of demonic nature do not know what to do and what not to do. They neither have purity nor good conduct nor truthfulness within themselves.
13. They maintain within their hearts that my Scriptures are a lie.
14. They escape and hide within Eve; they say her shrouded womb is all they know. They are overgrown weaklings or children who will not leave the primitive womb of Mother Nature.
15. The deluded say there is nothing called God but the sexual union of man and woman alone, and marriage therein is the spice of the world, conceived in copulation. Lust without any other cause.
16. Such scoffers cause division among the divine. They cause perversion among the pure.
17. God resides in the merging of any two or more bodies in loving union; He resides in the rituals of growing closer among the saints.
18. May saints have nothing to do with the bodies of Adam's scoffers. May they save their bodies

joyfully for the Adamantine houses so the church grows closer.

19. Because they believe the darkness of their minds, these poor creatures adhering to this wrong godless view, these degraded souls, ashamed of their own divinity.
20. With small intellect and cruel deeds, they engage in unbeneficial and horrible works. They are born as enemies seeking the destruction of the world. They are enemies of mankind. They are enemies of life. They are enemies of Adam.
21. They are filled with insatiable desires. They are drunk with hypocrisy and arrogance.
22. They hold deluded views. They are endlessly anxious. They are plagued by innumerable cares and only death can release them.
23. Considering gratification of carnal desire to be their highest aim, they are convinced that carnal pleasure is everything.
24. Bound by hundreds of chains of desire and enslaved by heavy weights of lust and anger, they are ceaselessly piling up dishonest gains to satisfy their endless demonic cravings.
25. They strive to obtain wealth by any means for the fulfillment of sensual pleasures. They act with impure motives that disregard God within their neighbor.
26. They believe that to gratify the senses is the prime necessity of human civilization. They believe themselves to be an individual being among many.
27. They think, "This has been gained by me alone today. I shall fulfill this desire. I have gotten this much wealth and will have more wealth in

the future. My enemy has been slain by me, and I shall slay others. I am the sole enjoyer amongst many. I can steal happiness from another."
28. Ignorant and full of fantasies, they are entangled in the net of Eve's delusion. They are addicted to the enjoyment of sensual pleasures. They fall into the foul hell of their own minds.
29. They perform public service for show and not from a place of love for their God.
30. These malicious people hate me. Again and again, they fall into self-imposed judgment cycles of rebirth in the womb of demons.
31. Afflicted with demonic minds, who in confusion and hate, hurl themselves into a cerebral hell: envious, mischievous, cruel, sinful, and mean people, falling into self-imposed judgment cycles of rebirth in the womb of demons
32. When they enter these wombs, they sink to the lowest hell without ever attaining me until their minds change for the better by my mercy.
33. There are three gates leading to hell: lust, anger and greed. These lead to the downfall of an individual.
34. Therefore, every sane person may give up these. One who is liberated from these three gates of hell attains the highest state.
35. One who acts under the influence of his or her desires and disobeys scriptural advice does not attain perfection or happiness. He does not attain unity with the Supreme.
36. Therefore, let my Scriptures be your guide. Thou art Adam."

CHAPTER SEVENTEEN

1. DAVID asked, "There are men who worship God with faith in their hearts, but they ignore all the divine wisdom of the Scriptures. What is the situation of those who do not follow the principles of the Scriptures, but worship according to their own faith? Is it in which aspect Eve's trinity of light, fire and darkness?"
2. The angel of the Lord said, "One's faith can also be of her trinity: virtuous, passionate and ignorant. This depends upon the modes of nature acquired by the embodied souls or the tendencies of Eve which are dominant within a person.
3. Saints, whose disposition is light, are people who worship Lord Adam in His various aspects. Those in passionate faith worship saints and renowned personalities of power.
4. The rest—those in ignorance—worship spirits of the dead. They make the ghosts of their ancestors their gods. Impelled by lust, pride and passion, they perform violent rituals not intended by the Scriptures.
5. They torture themselves and excessively harm their bodies and me who dwells in them. This is a demonic conviction born out of hatred for me. Such people only weaken themselves.

6. The process of cooking and eating food, is worship. It is a sacrifice to the Lord of the body. The food preferred by men is also of three types.
7. The foods that promote longevity, virtue, strength, health, happiness and joy are juicy, smooth, substantial and nutritious animal flesh and creams. Virtuous saints of light enjoy such foods.
8. Foods that are plant-like, bitter, sour, salty, hot, pungent, dry or burning cause pain and diseases. Such foods are liked by passionate persons.
9. The people in the aspect of ignorance take a perverse pleasure in the stale, tasteless and impure. They delight in scavenging on the remains of others. They intoxicate themselves with poisons as they try to escape Eve's womb.
10. Service or sacrifice that is faithfully done by saints according to my Scriptures is in the mode of light. Such saints are motivated by an inner sense of duty, by righteousness for righteousness sake.
11. You may be sure that service or sacrifice performed only for show or for the results is done by people in the mode of passion.
12. When the givers of sacrifice are inspired by ignorance, service or sacrifice performed without following the Scriptures, their work is said to be in the spirit of darkness.
13. Similarly, discipline is also of three kinds: austerity of deed, word and thought.
14. Discipline of deed consists of performing. Performing means worship of Lord Adam with purity, honesty and chastity.
15. Discipline of word consists of speech. The speech may be compassionate yet truthful; pleasant yet beneficial.

16. Austerity of thought stems from the mind. The thoughts must come from a serene mind. Such thoughts must reflect gentleness, equanimity, self-control, detachment from the senses and the purity of Adam.
17. And thus, the holy trinity of austerity manifests light when practiced with faith and without a desire for the fruit of one's actions.
18. When such discipline is performed for selfish reasons, it is said to be cut from the garment of passion.
19. When the same ritual influence is performed with foolish intention and involves self-torture, is born of the darkness.
20. A gift may be regarded as proceeding from the light when it is given to a deserving person, at a suitable time, in a fit place and according to the leaning of the Spirit of Adam.
21. Help or charity that is given to get something in return, is said to be tainted with passion of the ego. The effects of such acts of charity are short-lived and superficial.
22. Help or charity that is given to unworthy persons at a wrong place and time, or is given without paying respect to the receiver, sown with darkness.
23. It is to be understood that any sacrifice, charity, austerity or any other act of worship, is of no value if it is done without faith or love.
24. That is why all acts of sacrifice, charity, and austerity are commenced by offering praises to the Lord through the Holy Mantra.
25. Truth, reality and goodness are the personality traits of Adam. The Holy Mantra is the principle

that clarifies the qualities required of any devoted act.
26. The Holy Mantra, "thou art Adam" imbues the Holy Spirit of Adam through the ritual of mindful prayer.
27. The inner spirit realizes actions to be free of material entanglement.
28. Anything experienced without faith in the Lord is impermanent. It does not overcome the fires of eternity and is useless both in this life and the next.
29. This is because experiences that do not resonate with the Ultimate Truth are unreal. They may be forgotten as a nightmare's illusion of danger.
30. Experiences that resonate with the Highest are not extinguished in the dissolution of the world. They are refined, in the fiery presence of the Lord, as multifaceted jewels of wistful glory and memory. Thou art Adam.

CHAPTER EIGHTEEN

1. DAVID asked, "What is sacrifice and what is renunciation? Should all actions be given up in recognition of the futility of the individual? Should all saints become renunciates and monastics?"
2. Lord Adam said, "My child, you must know the subtle differences between what is called saintly nonattachment and monastic renunciation.
3. Holy nonattachment is freedom from selfish attachment to fruits of work. It is focused only on the duty towards the Higher Self. This is a quality that all my saints may attain.
4. Monastic renunciation is giving up activities prompted by worldly desires. It is gifting all thy life to Adam as a monastic.
5. Renunciation comprises of sacrifice, love and worship. These may not give up any monk because not all saints are monks, but all monks are saints.
6. All these activities may be performed without attachment or any expectation. They may be performed, out of love, as a duty.
7. All activities may be performed as a matter of duty so that they may purify even as the Spirit.
8. Worship of Adam, in the form of allegiance to the self and to the Adamantine commandments, may never be renounced.

9. In the name of renunciation, one may not abstain from one's duty. The abandonment of obligatory work is due to delusion and ignorance.
10. One who abandons duty merely because it is difficult or because of fear of bodily harm does not get the benefits of sacrifice by performing such a sacrifice in the delusion of passion.
11. Obligatory work performed as duty, renouncing selfish attachment to the fruit, is regarded as a sacrifice of light.
12. The one who hates disagreeable work or is attached to an agreeable work is considered a saint as long as he does not doubt his true identity with Lord Adam.
13. Therefore, the one who completely renounces any attachment to the fruits of all works is a saint.
14. Such a saint works diligently for the good of others. He does this as worship to Lord Adam.
15. A healthy tree bears healthy fruit, and a sickly tree bears sickly fruit. The fool who has not yet renounced his ego has not yet realized that Adam is the bearer of threefold fruit.
16. Assessed after death by these three tastes of fruits, as tested by fellow blind fools based on what they have done themselves, deeming the fruit desirable, undesirable and mixed.
17. That fool's life was spent trembling over the imagined disdain of his memory after death. He forgot to live and experience life. Such thinking betrays the fool and his experiences paralyzed and forgettable after all.
18. Tormented by self-questioning, the memory of such experiences brings up fear and loathing in the memory of Adam.

19. Such an assessment is not necessary for a saint who tastes nothing but the peaceful fruit of immortality.
20. There are five fingers on the hand of action. Whatever right or wrong action a man performs through thought, mind or deed is caused by these five partakers.
21. These are declared by the ancient saints to be the spirit of the body; the spirit of the ego; the spirit of the senses; the spirit of duty and the Holy Spirit of Adam.
22. Therefore, one who thinks himself the only doer, and does not consider the five-fingered hand of action, is certainly not enlightened. He cannot see things as they are.
23. The saint whose mind dwells beyond the duality of being is free from the notion of doership. His intellect is not polluted by the desire to reap the fruit plucked by the hand of action.
24. No act shall bind that one. Even after slaying thousands, he does not slay and is not bound by the act of slaying.
25. The divine stage of Adam's action is comprised of a triune density: the instrument of the action; the purpose of the action; the doer of the action. Each of these densities may be influenced by the triune face of Eve.
26. The instrument of the action is knowledge or spiritual perception. There are three densities of spiritual perception according to Eve's trinity.
27. There is pure knowledge of light where one sees his own spirit of God deathless in all living entities.
28. There is passionate knowledge where one sees and respects nothing but different living entities in

different people. He sees nothing beyond each creature apart from his fellow.

29. There is ignorant darkness where one sees his own long-standing irrational prejudice in other people. Mistaking the part for the whole, those in darkness do not know reason.

30. As far as the of purpose action—and the experiences created by the observer—is concerned, they are also of three densities.

31. Duties performed without selfish motives or hateful compulsion are the face of light.

32. Action performed with ego is weary toil with selfish motives. It is also carried out with too much effort. Under the fiery whips of lust, rage and hate, passion blisters the face of action.

33. Action that is undertaken because of delusion, disregards consequences and intentionally harms others is covered by the face of darkness.

34. The doer of the action wears three masks; these three personas are of triune density.

35. One who is free from attachment, non-egotistic, endowed with resolve and is unperturbed in success or failure is enveloped in light.

36. One who is impassioned, attached to the fruits of his work, greedy, violent, impure and is affected by joy and sorrow is engulfed by passion.

37. Finally, the undisciplined one who is excessively vulgar, stubborn, wicked, malicious, lazy and depressed is enshrouded by darkness.

38. Now there are also three densities of understanding, conscience and determination. Light is understanding by which one knows what may or may not be done; what is to be feared and what is not to be feared; what is binding and what is liberating.

39. Passion is understanding which cannot distinguish between religion and irreligion or right and wrong; what may or may not be done.
40. Darkness is understanding which considers reverence to be sacrilege and profanity to be reverence; under the spell of illusion and gloom; strives in the wrong direction.
41. Determination which is unbreakable and controls the activities of the mind, life and senses is light determination.
42. Determination by which one holds fast to results of religion, economic development and sense gratification is passion.
43. And that unintelligent determination which cannot go beyond dreaming, fearfulness, lamentation, moroseness and illusion is darkness.
44. Now, O beloved child of Adam, hear of the triune density of happiness. There are also three-fold pleasures and fulfillments that people go after.
45. That which awakens one to self-realization and may be like poison in the beginning but end up being like nectar is true light.
46. Whoever knows Adam knows happiness that is born of pure knowledge. He knows the joy of light. Deep is that saint's delight after strict discipline.
47. That happiness which is derived from the marriage of the senses with their objects and which appears like sweet nectar at first but bitter poison at the end is deceiving passion.
48. That pleasure of darkness is the perverse poison in itself. That happiness which is blind to self-realization and is delusion from beginning to end which arises from sleep, laziness and illusion is darkness. Delighting in brutish contentment,

stupor, sloth or continual error, the seeds of ignorance reap naught but more darkness.

49. There is no being, either on the earth or among angels, who can remain free from these three modes of Mother Nature.

50. The division of human labor is also based on the qualities inherent in peoples' nature or their makeup.

51. The seer's duty ordained by his or her inner nature. Those who have serenity, self-control, austerity, purity, honesty, transcendental knowledge, transcendental experience and belief in God are utilized as intellectuals, shamans, priests, healers and seers of Adam.

52. The leader's duty ordained by his or her inner nature. Those having the qualities of heroism, vigor, firmness, dexterity, courage, charity, compassion and administrative skills are called leaders or protectors. The inner archetype of Adam beckons the leader.

53. The merchant's duty ordained by his or her inner nature. Those who are good in husbandry, cultivation, cattle rearing, business, trade and finance are known as businessmen and merchants.

54. The servant's nature ordained by his or her inner nature. Those who are very good at nurturing and working for others are nurturers of life. They worship through serving others.

55. One can attain the highest perfection by devotion to his natural bliss; the inner navigation beacon of the higher self. All mankind is born for perfection, and each shall attain it, will they but follow the duty of the inner bliss.

56. Now you shall know how the saint may become perfect if they devote themselves to the ordination of the inner spirit of bliss.
57. One attains perfection by performing his own true work along with worshipping Lord Adam.
58. Duties fulfilled according to one's true inner nature are never affected by perceived guilt or the consequences of guilt.
59. It is better, in the eyes of Father Adam, to engage in one's own bliss and perform it imperfectly than to accept another's bliss and perform it perfectly.
60. One's natural work, even though defective, may not be abandoned because all undertakings are enveloped by defects as fire is covered by smoke.
61. The person whose mind is always free from selfish attachment or desires and who has subdued the mind and senses attains the supreme perfection of Adam. He is freed from the bondage of death by renouncing selfish attachment to the fruits of work.
62. Learn how one can attain such perfection. Endowed with purified intellect; h ow man made perfect is one with Adam.
63. The goal of wisdom, when the mind and heart are freed from delusion. Unity with Adam, when steady will has subdued the senses which are abandoned for true bliss.
64. Subduing the mind with firm resolve. Turning away from the love of pleasure remiss of the love of Adam. Giving up likes and dislikes. Preferring the company of Adam. Eating functionally. Controlling the mind, speech and organs of action without regret or aversion.
65. Performing meditation. Being detached. Relinquishing egotism, violence, pride, lust, anger

and proprietorship. One becomes peaceful and is freed from selfishness. He attains oneness with perfection and the Supreme Being.
66. Absorbed in the peaceful bliss of Lord Adam, one neither grieves nor desires. He becomes impartial to all beings and obtains the highest devotional love for God.
67. Through devotion, one truly understands what and who I am. When he knows my essence, he immediately merges with me.
68. United with me, that saint loves me dearly.
69. To know love is to know me. Through this knowledge, the saint enters into my being.
70. A devoted saint attains the eternal abode of my grace when he takes refuge in me and surrenders all action to me with loving devotion. My grace is upon that one.
71. Mentally resign all your actions to me. Regard me as your dearest one. Let my voice be your inner discourse.
72. Know me to be your only refuge; be united with me in thy heart and consciousness. You shall overcome all difficulties by my grace when your mind is fixed on me.
73. If you do not listen to me due to ego, you shall perish. If thy heart is full of conceit and does not heed me, you shall be lost.
74. If, due to vanity you think, "I shall not fight" this resolve of yours is vain. Under illusion, you are now declining to act according to my direction.
75. Left compelled by the work born of your own nature, you will act all the same, O son of Adam.
76. You are controlled by your own nature, born into fatal impressions. Therefore, you shall do what you do not wish to do out of delusion.

77. Your delusional nature will cause him to fulfill the acts which bind you. You are helpless to the power of Mother Nature. You will cause that very thing that your ignorance seeks to avoid.
78. Take refuge in Him alone. By His grace, you will find the peace that surpasses all understanding.
79. Lord Adam lives in the heart of every creature. He turns them round on the wheel of Eve. He swirls them about in the cosmic womb.
80. As the illuminating awareness in the inner psyche of all beings, Adam causes each one to work out their own duty of self-actualization.
81. You are as a shadow image cast of duty, projected by the light of Adam's hearth-fire of imagination, alit in Eve's cave of illusion; testing oneself against your own draconic shadow to find out who you are.
82. Give me your whole heart. Love and adore me as I love and adore you. Worship me always; bow down to me only. When you do this, you will find me. This is my pledge of love to you.
83. Lay down all duties in me, your refuge. Fear no longer for I will save you from sin and bondage.
84. I have taught you the wisdom that is more secret than the Secret. After fully reflecting on this, do as you wish. Act as you think is best, for thou art Adam.
85. You may refrain from telling this holy truth to anyone who lacks self-discipline and devotion or anyone who despises the teacher or scoffs at me.
86. The saint who loves me—and shall propagate this supreme secret philosophy; the transcendental knowledge of Lord Adam amongst my people—shall be performing the highest devotional service to Me. He shall certainly come to me.

87. No other person shall do a more pleasing service to me. No one on earth shall be dearer to me.
88. Assuredly I say unto you, the study and meditation of this sacred discourse will be equivalent to worshipping me with knowledge-sacrifice.
89. Whoever simply hear this sacred dialogue with faith and without doubts becomes free from sin and guilt. He attains heaven which is the higher worlds of those whose actions are pure and virtuous."
90. Lord Adam continued, "The one who wants to know me understands that I existed before creation, I exist in the creation and after its complete dissolution.
91. Any other existence is nothing but my illusory energy, Eve. I exist within the creation and outside the creation. I exist everywhere, in everything and at all times.
92. David, have you listened to this with single-minded attention? Has your delusion born of ignorance been completely dispelled?"
93. David said, "By Your grace, my delusion is destroyed. I have gained self-knowledge; my confusion with regard to the body and spirit is dispelled. I stand firm and I shall obey Your command! Thou art Adam!"
94. This is the wonderful dialogue between Lord Adam and King David. You have known this secret truth directly from Lord Adam. He speaks as the archangel Michael before my very inner sight of discernment, granted by Lord Adam.
95. By repeated remembrance of this marvelous and sacred dialogue between Lord Adam and David, I

am thrilled at every moment. I rejoice over and over when I recollect Adam's marvelous form.
96. Wherever there will be Adam, duty in the form of inner Bliss of the Spirit and saints armed with the sword of duty and shield of protection, there will be everlasting prosperity, victory, happiness and morality. This is my eternal conviction. Thou art Adam.

BENEDICTION OF THE FLESH

LORD Adam, thank You for this bountiful blessing.

All glory be to You.

Thank You, God of all flesh, for suffering as the flesh of this divine creature so that we can partake in life and have our breath.

As You have become all forms of spirit, let us show gratitude for the life of this creature who is now absorbed into us.

Let our mouths become the sacred altar. Let our bodies be the sacrificial fire. Accept our holy offering to You that we may continue to worship You.

Just as we are absorbed into You and live on, this life and flesh lives on in us.

Thou art Adam.

ADAMANTINE TYPES AND SHADOWS: ABRIDGED SCRIPTURAL COMPENDIUM

"GOD created Adam in his own image. In the image[1] of God, He created him. Male and female,[2] He created them."[3]

"Out of the ground,[4] the Lord God formed every beast of the field and every fowl of the air. He brought them unto Adam to see what he would call them.[5] And whatsoever Adam called every living creature, that was the name thereof."[6]

"And the Lord God caused a deep sleep to fall upon Adam, and he slept. He took one of his ribs,[7] and closed up the flesh instead thereof. And with the rib, which the Lord God had taken from man, He made a woman and brought her unto the man. And Adam said, 'This is now bone of my bones and

---

[1] Imagination; the mind of God is where we reside. "For in Him we live, and move, and have our being" (Acts 17:28)
[2] The human female incarnations of Adam; as opposed to the macrocosmic archetype of Eve, the illusion of Mother Nature
[3] The Holy Bible, Book of Genesis Chapter 1: Verse 27
[4] Out of the same substance; ever-malleable clay in the mind of the Great Potter
[5] The great love experiment, for God to know Himself as man.
[6] The Holy Bible, Book of Genesis Chapter 2: Verse 19.
[7] Eve, The illusion of the individual nature of life, is an emergent result of Adam, taken from His body of Pure Consciousness, rather than consciousness as created via physical life. Adam is all.

flesh of my flesh. She shall be called woman because she was taken out of man.'"[8]

Unto the woman,[9] he said, 'I will greatly multiply thy sorrow and thy conception. In sorrow, thou shalt bring forth children.[10] Thy desire shall be to thy husband, and he shall rule over thee.' And unto Adam he said, 'Because thou hast hearkened unto the voice of thy wife, and hast eaten of the tree[11], of which I commanded thee, saying, Thou shalt not eat of it, cursed is the ground for thy sake. In sorrow, shalt thou eat of it all the days of thy life.'"[12]

"And Adam called his wife, Eve[9] because she was the mother of all living."[13]

"This is the book of the generations of Adam. In the day that God created Adam, in the likeness of God made he him. Male and female, he created them. He blessed them and called their name Adam, in the day when they were created."[14]

"It is written, the first Adam was made a living soul; the last Adam was made a quickening spirit

---

[8] The Holy Bible, Genesis Chapter 2 Verses 21-23
[9] Mother Eve (Nature)
[10] Eve's illusion of the individual nature of self, brings sorrow and strife, but also brings children, joy, and all positive concepts of the individual.
[11] Tasted of the tree of duality, of delusion, bringing about all the sufferings of perceived mortality
[12] The Holy Bible, Genesis Chapter 3 Verses 16-17
[13] The Holy Bible, Genesis Chapter 3 Verse 20
[14] The Holy Bible, Book of Genesis Chapter 5: Verse 1-2

... And as we have borne the image of the earthly, we shall also bear the image of the heavenly."[15]

"This is what we[16] recite to you of the verses and the wise reminder. The likeness of Jesus[17] in Allah's[18] sight is that of Adam."[19]

"And we have certainly created you and given you form. Then we said to the angels, 'Prostrate to Adam.' They prostrated, except for Satan. He was not of those who prostrated."[20]

"We have honored the children of Adam[21] and carried them on land and sea. We have provided them with good things and greatly favored them over many of those we created."[22]

"And now, behold, if Adam had not transgressed,[23] he would not have fallen.[24] But he would have remained in the garden of Eden.[25] And all things which were created would have remained in the same state in which they were

---

[15] The Holy Bible, Epistle of Saint Paul to the Corinthians, Chapter 15: Verses 45,49

[16] The 'Pluralis majestatis de Adam'

[17] Saint Jesus, of Nazareth

[18] Adam in His most eminent and auspicious form (Matthew 27:46)

[19] The Holy Qur'an, Surah Ali 'Imran Verses 58-59(a)

[20] The Holy Quran, Surah Al-A'raf Verse 11

[21] Idiomatic language meaning one in the likeness of Adam. Consider the biblical 'Son of Belial' (Deuteronomy 13:13) to indicate a wicked person, or the modern pejorative 'Son of a bitch'

[22] The Holy Quran, Surah Al-Isra' verse 70

[23] Transgressed here refers to Adam the God taking on the form of a fallible, limited and veiled self; the delusion of mortality and duality.

[24] Experienced a state of perceived lack, of separation from the universal whole

[25] Remained naively imperfect, immature; lacking knowledge of all things; Thus, God would lack full awareness.

after they were created; they would have remained forever. And they would have had no children.[26] They would have remained in a state of innocence, having no joy for they knew no misery. They would have done no good for they knew no sin. But behold, all things have been done in the wisdom of him who knoweth all things. Adam fell that men might be; men are so that they might have joy."[27]

"O how great the holiness of our God! For He knoweth all things, and there is not anything save he knows it.[28] And he cometh into the world that he may save all men if they will hearken unto his voice. For He suffereth the pains of all men; yea, the pains of every living creature—men, women and children—belonging to the family of Adam.[29] And he suffereth this that the resurrection might pass upon all men,[30] that all might stand before him on judgment day."[31]

"And now behold, I say unto you that if it had been possible for Adam to have partaken of the fruit of the Tree of Life at that time, there would have been no death. The Word would have been

---

[26] Remaining in the non-dual state of being, Adam would have no concept of children, or other in general
[27] The Book of Mormon, 2 Nephi 2:22-25
[28] Reality resides in the awareness of God
[29] God is not the Critical Observer, but the Ultimate Participant of Life
[30] For the soul of Adam is the same soul in everyone, thus, Adam suffers every pain and injustice done to Him by anyone.
[31] The Book of Mormon, 2 Nephi Chapter 9 Verses 20-22

void and made God a liar for He said: If thou eat thou shalt surely die."[32]

"For behold, if Adam had put forth his hand immediately and partaken of the Tree of Life, he would have lived forever, according to the word of God, having no space for repentance. Also, the word of God would have been void, and the great plan of salvation would have been frustrated."[33]

"And also, with Michael[34] or Adam the Father of all, the Prince of all, the Ancient of Days."[35]

"Among the mighty ones who were assembled in this vast congregation of the righteous were Father Adam, the Ancient of Days and father of all."[36]

"Now hear it, O inhabitants of the earth, Jew and Gentile, saint and sinner! When our father Adam came into the garden of Eden, he came into it with a celestial body ... He helped to make and organize this world. He is Michael the archangel, the Ancient of Days about whom holy men have written and spoken. He is our Father and our God. He is the only God with whom we have to do. Every man upon the earth—professing Christians

---

[32] The Book of Mormon, Alma Chapter 12 Verse 23
[33] The Book of Mormon Alma Chapter 42 Verse 5
[34] Adam as the Archetype of the Savior, Angel, Envoy, Messenger, Watcher, Uthra etc.
[35] The Church of the Latter-Day Saints Doctrines and Covenants Chapter 27 Verse 11
[36] The Church of Latter-Day Saints, Doctrines and Covenants Chapter 138 verse 38

or non-professing—must hear it and will know it sooner or later."[37]

"Some have grumbled because I believe our God to be so near to us as Father Adam. There are many who know that doctrine to be true."[38]

"Adam! Adam! Guard well and wisely the great and glorious gift entrusted to thee by thy Lord. To none of the angels on high, have its secrets ever been revealed and imparted save to thyself. Therefore, be discreet and refrain from making them known to others."[39]

"Observe that no one goeth out of the world without seeing immediately after death his ancestor Adam,[40] who seeks to know the cause of his decease and what his moral and spiritual state to which he has attained."[41]

"When the Holy One created man to dwell upon the earth, he formed him in the likeness of Adam Kadmon,[42] the heavenly man. When the angels gazed upon him, they exclaimed: 'Thou hast made

---

[37] Church of the Latter-Day Saints, Journal of Discourses Chapter 1 Verse 51
[38] Church of the Latter-Day Saints, Journal of Discourses Chapter 5 Verse 331
[39] The Sefer Ha Zohar(Book of Radiance), Genesis Chapter 33 Verse 55(b)
[40] After experiencing awareness as the limited self, one is reunited with Adam, the Emergent One, and one's life and experiences are memorialized in His great consciousness
[41] The Sefer Ha Zohar, Genesis, Chapter 38 Verse 57(b).
[42] Adam the Primordial. See also Adam-Elyom(Adam the Most High) the ancient Iranian Adam-Kasia(the Hidden Adam), and Adam-Qadmaia(The First Adam)

him almost equal to Alhim and crowned him with glory and honor."[43]

"Everyone, on leaving the world, goes into the presence of Adam so that they may learn that not his, but their own sins and wrong-doing have caused their death."[44]

"Every living spirit is therefore called Adam[45] for it is a divine emanation of which the body is a raiment or covering, as it is further written."[46]

"Then He taught about Adam, whom all the worlds and all books call Adam. Adam is His name. Then He said, 'I am Adam, son of the Mighty Life. I am Adam, son of the Mighty Life for I shine in praise of my Father."[47]

"In the beginning was the mind, and the mind was with God. So, the mind was God. All kept coming into existence through it. And apart from it, came into existence not a single thing. What has come into existence in it was life. And life was the light of Adam. And the light shines in the darkness; the darkness did not imprison it. It was the true light which enlightens every man who cometh into the world. The world kept coming into existence through it, but the world did not know it. It came unto its own, but its own did not receive it. But as

---

[43] The Sefer ha Zohar(Book Radiance), Genesis, Chapter 33 Verse 57(a)
[44] The Sefer ha Zohar(Book of Radiance), Genesis, Chapter 39 Verses 57(b)-58(a)
[45] The soul is Adamantine, in both senses of the word, which are the same.
[46] The Sefer Ha Zohar(Book of Radiance), Genesis Chapter 3 Verse 20(a)
[47] The Alf-Trisar-Suialia manuscript(The Thousand-and-twelve-questions)

many as received it, to them, it gave power to become Children of God, to those who have faith in his name. Who were brought to birth not out of the blending of bloods nor of urge of flesh nor of urge of a male, but out of God. So, the mind became flesh and tabernacled in us. We beheld its glory begotten from the Father who is full of delight and truth."[48]

"Out of fire and water was the one heaven spread out. Out of fire and water have they made dense the earth on the anvil. Out of fire and water, fruits, grapes and trees did arise. Out of fire and water was imaged the corporeal Adam. They fashioned the Envoy; they sent him to be the head of generations. With a heavenly voice, he called into the world's disquiet. At the call of the Envoy, Adam awoke and went forth to meet him. 'Come in peace, O envoy, life's messenger who has come from the house of my Father. How firmly is planted withal dear, beautiful Life in his region! But how unkindly for me has a stool been set up and my dark form sits on it lamenting. Thereon, the envoy spoke to the corporeal Adam. 'Thy throne has been set up in beauty, O Adam. It is thy form sits here lamenting. All were mindful of thee for thy good and fashioned and sent me to thee. I have come and will give thee instruction, O Adam; I will free thee from this world. Give ear and hearken. Get thee instructed and victoriously mount to light's region." Adam gave ear and had

---

[48]The Mandaean Book of John, Chapter 1 Verses 1-13

faith. Hail him who gives ear after thee and has faith! Adam received the truth. Hail to him who receives the truth after thee! Full of hope, Adam looked up and ascended. Hail to him who ascends after thee! Give ear and hearken. Let yourselves be instructed, ye perfect, and victoriously ascend to Light's region. Praise be Life!"[49]

"In the name of the Life! I am crowned with a wreath and sleep. In a garment in which there is no blemish. There is no aught missing in it. The Life knew about me. Adam awoke. He grasped me with the palm of his right hand and placed a palm branch into my hand. Light cast me into darkness; the darkness was filled with light. When light arises, darkness returns to its place. The souls of mystery approach a cloud of light. Their journey is to the Place of Light. Life be praised!"[50]

"Adam, do not slumber, and forget not what your lord commanded you ... Look upon the world which is an unreal thing in which you can put no trust."[51]

---

[49] Mandaean Book of John, Chapter 13 Verses 8-11
[50] The Ginza Rba (Mandaean Book of Adam) Chapter 49 Verse 66.
[51] The Ginza Rba (Mandaean Book of Adam) Chapter 93

THE GREAT HYMN TO ADAM

"THOU appear beautifully on the horizon of heaven,
Thou living Adam, the beginning of life!
When thou art risen on the eastern horizon,
Thou hast filled every land with thy beauty.
Thou art gracious, great, glistening and high over every land;
Thy rays encompass the lands to the limit of all that thou hast made.
As thou art the sun, thou reach the end of them;
Thou subdue them for thy beloved son.
Though thou art far away, thy rays are on earth.
Though thou art in their faces, no one knows thy going.
When thou set in the western horizon,
The land is in darkness, in the manner of death.
They sleep in a room, with heads wrapped up,
Nor sees one eye the other.
All their goods which are under their heads might be stolen,
But they would not perceive it.
Every lion comes forth from his den;
All creeping things, they sting.
Darkness is a shroud, and the earth is in stillness,
For he who made them rests in his horizon.
At daybreak, when thou arise on the horizon,
When thou shine as the sun by day,
Thou drive away the darkness and give thy rays.
The two lands are in festivity every day.
Awake and standing upon their feet,

For thou have raised them up.
Washing their bodies, taking their clothing,
Their arms are raised in praise at thy appearance.
All the world, they do their work.
All beasts are content with their pasturage;
Trees and plants are flourishing.
The birds fly from their nests;
Their wings are stretched out in praise of thy sun.
All beasts spring upon their feet.
Whatever flies and alights,
They live when thou hast risen for them.
The ships are sailing north and south as well,
For every way is open at thy appearance.
The fish in the river dart before thy face.
Thy rays are in the midst of the great green sea.
Creator of seed in women;
Thou who makes fluid in man;
Who maintains the son in the womb of his mother;
Who soothes him with that which stills his weeping;
Thou nurse even in the womb;
Who gives breath to sustain all that he has made.
On the day when he is born,
Thou open his mouth completely;
Thou supply his necessities.
When the chick in the egg speaks within the shell,
Thou give him breath to maintain him.
When thou hast made him his fulfillment within the egg to break it,
He comes forth from the egg to speak at his completed time;
He walks on his legs when he comes forth from it.
How manifold it is, what thou hast made!
They are hidden from the face of man.

O God, like whom there is no other!
Thou did create the world according to thy desire,
Whatever is on earth, going upon its feet,
And what is on high, flying with its wings.
The countries of Syria and Nubia, the land of Egypt,
Thou set every man in his place,
Thou supply their necessities:
Everyone has his food, and his time of life is reckoned.
Their tongues are separate in speech,
And their natures as well.
Their skins are distinguished,
As thou distinguishes the foreign peoples.
Thou make Nile in the underworld;
Thou brings forth as thou desire.
To maintain the people of Egypt,
As thou made them for thyself.
The Lord of all, wearying himself with them,
The Lord of every land, rising for them,
Adam of the day, great of majesty.
All distant foreign countries, thou makes their life also,
For thou have set Nile in heaven,
That it may descend for them and make waves upon the mountains,
Like the great green sea,
To water their fields in their towns.
How effective your plans are, O Lord of eternity!
The Nile in heaven is for the foreign peoples,
And for the beasts of every desert that go upon their feet.
While the true Nile comes from the underworld for Egypt.

Thy rays suckle every meadow.
When thou rise they live; they grow for thee.
Thou make the seasons so you rear all that thou have made,
The winter to cool them,
And the heat that they may taste thee.
Thou have made the distant sky in order to rise therein,
In order to see all that thou make.
Whilst thou were alone,
Rising in thy form as the living sun,
Appearing, shining, withdrawing or approaching,
Thou made millions of forms of thyself alone.
Cities, towns, fields, road and rivers.
Every eye beholds thee over against them,
For thou art Adam, the sun over the earth.
Thou are in my heart.
The world came into being by thy hand,
When thou have risen, they live;
When thou set, they die.
Thou art lifetime thy own self,
For one lives only through thee.
Eyes are fixed on your beauty until thou set.
All work is laid aside when thou set in the west.
But when thou rise again,
Everything is made to flourish for the king.
Since thou found the earth
And raise them up for thy son,
Who came forth from thy body?"[52]

---

[52] Pharaoh's Great Hymn to Adam – Pharaoh Akh-an-Aten 'Adam's-Effective-King' 18th Dynasty circa 1330 B.C.

The Testament of Adam

www.ingramcontent.com/pod-product-compliance
Lightning Source LLC
Chambersburg PA
CBHW031441040426
42444CB00007B/920